The Mystical 10
Prospering with Ten Powerful Spiritual Principles

Don Welsh, D.D.

Copyright © 2014 Don Welsh

All rights reserved.

ISBN-13: 9780692209004
ISBN-10: 069220900X

DEDICATION

To Rev. LaVonne Rae Andrews/Welsh
for her loving encouragement and support
of the other passion in my life.

CONTENTS

Appreciation   g

Introduction   Pg. #1

Overview   Pg. #3

1   Genesis   Pg. #8

2   Gratitude   Pg #18

3   Guiltless   Pg #28

4   Goodness   Pg #42

5   Gladness   Pg #59

6   Guidance   Pg #75

7   Goals   Pg #91

8   Growth   Pg #105

9   Game Plan   Pg #118

10   Givingness   Pg #127

ACKNOWLEDGMENTS

Thanks to Wil Welsh, the first writer in the family,
to Laura Kepner who was a great example to her Dad,
and to the North San Luis Obispo County
Writer's group of the Morro Bay Library.

The Mystical 10

Prospering with 10 Powerful Spiritual Principles

Don Welsh, D.D.

Introduction

You can increase your level of prosperity by learning and employing the ten ancient spiritual principles described in this book. By exploring the ten concepts and using the ten tools included here, your life can be transformed and you will live more abundantly than ever before in ten weeks or less. My advice is that you read a chapter per week and practice the assigned suggestions, so that after ten weeks you will have gained the knowledge and experienced the exercises (tools) in depth. Of course, the pace is a personal choice and you are free to take less or more time to complete this "class" in prosperous living. There are no tests to pass, yet by the end of the book, you will have your license to thrive – your "thriver's license" so to speak. The principles of prosperity included here will enhance your level of expressing life in many areas. Prosperity author and teacher, Catherine Ponder, claims,

"You are prosperous to the degree you are experiencing peace, health and plenty in your world."

- Catherine Ponder, *Open Your Mind to Prosperity*

The Mystical Ten focuses on spiritual principles of prosperity so that you will undoubtedly become wealthier in your financial affairs. In addition, as you apply the principles, you will most likely improve your level of wellness, wisdom and love. Every area of your life will be affected positively.

Of course, you will want to participate fully by practicing the principles as suggested by the assignments at the end of each chapter including tracking your progress by noting the "wins" you will experience daily.

Overview

The Mystical Ten provides information about ten prosperity principles all beginning with the letter "G" and explained within each chapter. The capital letter "G" roughly resembles a spiral. The ancient Mayans drew an image similar to "G" when they wanted to symbolize Hunab Ku, their universal god of movement and measure. I will use words starting with "G" to represent the ten spiritual principles of prosperity.

The ten "G" words or phrases representing the principles are:

Genesis

Gratitude

Guiltless

Goodness

Gladness

Guidance

Goals

Growth

Game Plan

Givingness

Genesis means the beginning, appropriately. We will investigate the Source, where it all begins, which is God (or Hunab Ku, Allah, Great Spirit, Creator, Lord, Universal Mind, the Infinite or whatever word you prefer.) The spiritual tool I will teach is meditation, because it is through a deep inner connection with God that we come to know and understand that God is the Source of prosperity and the *only* source. I will suggest entering into meditation gently by meditating only two minutes per day for a week and increasing your meditation time two minutes daily each week, so that it will be twenty minutes at the end of ten weeks.

The second chapter is Gratitude, in which we will explore the prospering power of giving thanks. The spiritual tool included will be affirmations. You will create a personal affirmation for yourself and repeat it frequently on a daily basis.

Guiltless is the subject of the third chapter and it is about your worthiness as a Being of Light. You deserve to live life abundantly, yet somehow you may have unconsciously accepted a false belief that there is something wrong with you. There may be a need to forgive yourself or others, and you will learn to journal as a spiritual tool.

Chapter four focuses on Goodness. We will become convinced that prosperity is good and specifically, money is good. For the spiritual tool, I will teach a simplified form of positive prayer that you may learn to use daily.

Gladness is the subject of chapter five. Are you "glad" to go to work (or whatever your life activities may be)? Do you have enthusiasm? A fun tool called mind mapping will be included as the tool to be used.

The sixth spiritual principle is guidance, which is all about listening to "that still small voice" within. You will tap into the Genius Mind through the spiritual tool called Visioning.

Seventh, we will discuss Goals. It is important to declare your intentions, to delineate your desires and to announce your expectations. The spiritual tool we will review and use is goal setting.

The word for chapter eight is Growth. The universe is expanding, so there is a natural tendency for growth and expansion to take place. Visualization as a spiritual technique will enhance your acceptance of expansive prosperity.

For chapter nine, we will create a Game plan. Expansion happens automatically when there is order and balance in our finances and our lives. A simplified budgeting or financial planning procedure that I prefer to call your game plan becomes the spiritual tool included in the chapter's lesson.

Finally, in chapter ten, I will discuss Givingness. We have all heard that as we give, so also shall we receive. Yet this simple teaching has been tainted by confusion due to the associated guilt that clergy and others have attached to giving. The principle of tithing is a wonderful tool to prosper oneself. It is not done for the purpose of prospering a church or religious organization, although that could well be an inherent result. Tithing means *ten*. It is an ancient practice in which people give ten percent of their income to the Source through the source of their spiritual nurturing. So the spiritual tool I will teach is tithing.

You may have heard the story about a minister who was asked to inform an elderly man that he had inherited a million dollars. People were afraid the old guy would get so excited, he would have a heart attack. So the minister approached the subject gently. He asked, "What would you do if you inherited a million dollars?" The old guy replied, "I would tithe on it. Lets see, that's one hundred thousand dollars to your church, Reverend." The minister had a heart attack.

For many people, it seems difficult to suddenly jump into the practice of tithing. Notice your own reaction when you came across the "T" word. No matter how convinced you may have become of the validity of tithing, it is one giant step for humankind! Therefore, I suggest working up to giving ten percent. Start in the first week, or during the period of time you are reading the first chapter, and give one percent of what you receive. For each chapter, increase your donations to a source of your spiritual nurturing by one percent, so that you are giving two percent, then three, four and eventually ten percent, a true tithe.

Chapter One

Genesis

Principle: God

Tool: Meditation

One Sunday morning, a minister was preoccupied with concerns about how to ask her congregation to come up with more money for repairs to the church building. So, she was annoyed that the regular organist was sick and a substitute had been brought in at the last minute. The substitute asked what he should play.

"Here's a copy of the order of service, the minister said impatiently. "But you will have to think of something to play after I make the announcement about finances."

During the service, the minister paused and said, "Brothers and sisters, we are in great difficulty; the roof repairs cost twice as much as we expected, and we need $4,000 more. Any of you who can pledge one hundred dollars or more, please stand up."

At that moment, the organist played "The Star Spangled Banner." And that is how the substitute organist became the permanent organist.

A successful church knows that there is really only one Source of their supply – God. And a prosperous person knows that god is the only Source of their supply. It is not the job, the business, the inheritance or the lottery. Those may all be vehicles through which God provides, but none of them is the Source Itself. The ancient prophets knew where their abundance came from:

"And the Lord shall enrich you in good things, in the fruit of your body and in the bearing of your cattle and in the fruit of your ground, in the land which the Lord swore to your fathers to give you. The Lord shall open to you his good storehouse, the heaven, to give you rain to your land in its season; and he will bless all the works of your hands..."

- Deuteronomy 28:11-12

The Lord (meaning I Am That I Am) was and is the only Source. So why have we questioned our Source? Maybe it's because God is invisible and we may find it difficult to trust something we cannot experience with our five senses. What we can experience, however, is that which *results* from the creative activity of Spirit. Just as a scientist cannot see the principle she is investigating, she can see the out picturing of the activity of the principle. We can see the effect that gravity has on our world, even though we cannot see the law of gravity itself. We can conduct experiments, just like a scientist, and discover the hidden laws that govern our world. We call such experiments *life.* As you apply the spiritual principles of prosperity included in each chapter by using the tools that apply, you will demonstrate the validity of the principles. And, incidentally, your level of prosperity will increase. As that happens, you will actually be building up your faith in the invisible Source. And you know what faith can do:

"If there is faith in you even as a grain of mustard seed, you will say to this mountain, move away from here, and it will move away; and nothing would prevail over you."

- Matthew 17:20

By the way, mustard seeds are miniscule. So it is just a little faith that can move mountains – the mountains we have made out of molehills, mainly. These are the mental and emotional barriers that we have placed in our own way.

We live in an unlimited, boundless, abundant universe. As American philosopher and founder of the New Thought movement called "The Science of Mind," Dr. Ernest Holmes wrote:

"We see abundance in the Universe. We cannot count the grains of seed on a single beach. The earth contains untold riches, and the very air is vibrant with power."

- *The Science of Mind* 28.3

During a wet weather cycle in California called an El Nino, I was living in the wettest place in the state – Boulder Creek, near Big Basin State Park in the Santa Cruz Mountains. All the rain has created beautiful old redwood forests filled with ferns and all sorts of greenery. The downside was that every now and then the ground would get so saturated that it would cause mudslides. I had a first hand experience with a mudslide.

One rainy night, the children were asleep as I relaxed in the family room. I could hear the normal sound of rushing water in the stream called Boulder Creek, which ran through the middle of the property. In the summertime, it was a babbling brook, but in the winter it turned into a raging current.

Suddenly I was jarred by a crashing sound. I thought a tree had fallen on the house, so I ran up to the third story looking for damage, but fortunately, there was no tree poking through the ceiling. I went back downstairs and opened a door overlooking the creek. Below me was a chasm. A mudslide had removed the backyard terracing and a tree and landscaping had been swept down the river. One leg of the deck was dangling. With the small retaining wall that had supported it gone, the deck seemed to levitating on its own.

Unsure of the extent of the problem, we spent the night in the home of some friends nearby. The next day, I inspected the damage. While the house was safe for now, a new retaining wall and support for the deck would need to be constructed. I knew the cost would be more than our finances could bear.

I had been trained to become a licensed Practitioner or spiritual counselor, so I prayed for abundance, for the solution to the repair problems and for the perfect outcome for the highest good.

When the town was declared a disaster area, I knew there would be inexpensive loans available and I applied. At the same time, I filed a claim to our homeowner's insurance company. As I waited for action, I heard that everyone in similar situations was being turned down for settlements from insurance because mudslides are out of doors.

Reluctantly, I proceeded with a loan, even though the payments were going to be difficult to handle. Having released all expectations about insurance coverage, I was surprised when I received a phone call informing me that my claim had gone to the top – the board of the insurance company – where the decision was made to pay my claim. It seems my case was unique because the dangling deck was connected to the house and the house was covered. They paid more than $50,000 for a huge retaining wall, a new deck and even a stairway all the way down to the creek, which hadn't even been there before.

Five years later, when I became a minister and needed to sell the house in order to relocate, the increased value to the property from the improvements made it possible to sell the house in a "buyers" market for the amount needed to retrieve the original investment, pay selling costs, and cover the costs of moving. I learned to trust God to provide and to do it in a manner that might be much better than I could imagine it to be.

Prosperity teacher, Edwene Gaines says:

"The inexhaustible Resource of Spirit is equal to every demand. There is no reality in lack. Abundance is here and now manifest."

- Edwene Gaines

Manifest means it is here already. You do not have to wait around for it, unless you believe you do. God is infinite and provides all that we require to live fully right now. And we are meant to live abundantly:

"I have come that they might have life, and have it abundantly."

- John 10:10

Why is this so? As it is written,

"God is love."

- I John 4:8

And this divine love is the self-givingness of Spirit. The One desires only to give. The Universe is on your side. God wants you to prosper. Compare it to a newspaper notice from a bank trying to locate a long lost client with money in their account. If no one comes forward, the funds will just sit there collecting interest until the money is transferred to the state. The Creator wants you to claim you good. Ernest Holmes wrote,

"My belief is that God not only *loves* a prosperous (person), but that we discredit both Him and ourselves when we experience poverty!"

- Ernest Holmes, *It's Up to You*

Another great New Thought teacher, the co-founder of the Unity movement, Charles Fillmore, wrote,

""The Father's desire for us is unlimited good, not merely the means of a meager existence. We cannot be poor. It is a sin to be poor."

- Charles Fillmore, *Prosperity*

Because of the all-loving nature of the Universe, the Divine supports whatever is the highest and best for all. In all likelihood, Spirit does not support what is right for only one person. Activities that align with universal good, cannot fail. Activities based upon greed and selfishness cannot succeed.

"No good thing will He withhold from them that walk uprightly."

- Psalm 84:11

To walk uprightly would be to choose activities that are for the good of all. Then success is guaranteed.

Spiritual Tool – Meditation

Meditation is an excellent way to be convinced of the Presence of the higher Power. I feel the primary purpose of meditation is to feel a sense of oneness with Spirit.

There are as many techniques of meditation as there are teacher of it, and all of them have something beneficial to offer. My intention is to keep it simple. If you have already adopted meditation techniques that work for you, that's great. You do not need to change, so long as you are feeling Oneness when you meditate.

The ancient Hindu meditators taught students to focus on their breathing. With each in- breath, they formed a word that sounded like sucking in breath; "hum". With each out-breath, they said, "sah" which seems to sound like releasing breath. They would follow the breath in and out saying to themselves, "hum" and "sah". As they progressed in their ability to focus, they reached a point in which they felt oneness and felt the Presence between "hum" and sah". At the place where the in-breath ceases and the out-breath begins. They called this point, "Om" or more precisely, "Aum". Would you like to stop reading and try this simple technique for two minutes right now? You might like to play some quiet background music while you meditate. I find it useful in keeping my attention on the meditation. Some find music distracting. So, do what is most effective for you.

Whenever you meditate, make sure you are seated or lying in a comfortable position, so that you are not distracted by aches, tension or bodily sensations. You do not need to sit in any particular position, such as the lotus position with your legs folded under you and your arms outstretched. But that is certainly okay. I hold my head high, as if a string is attached to it from the ceiling or sky. My spinal column is straight and my arms and legs unfolded so that it feels as if a free flow of energy moves thought my body. I place my feet flat on the floor in order to feel grounded.

Close your eyes so that they are not pulled to anything moving in your environment or focus on one object such as a candle or flower.

To experiment with "hum" and "sah", focus on your breath as it comes in and say "hum" to yourself. Breathe out saying "sah". Continue for a minute saying the words over and over. Then see if you can locate that place between "hum" and "sah" and say "Om" to yourself for a minute. You've become a two-minute meditator.

As you read this book, you may choose to increase your meditation time by two minute increments, staying focused on "Om" and on your connection with the Divine. Allow time to gently reawaken to the outer world.

At first, it is more important to do a tiny bit of meditating every day, rather than one or two long meditations during the week, so that you build up a daily habit of meditation.

Assignments

1. Meditate at least two minutes daily using the breathing technique described in this chapter or any other meditation technique you like.

2. Write down a "win' – something positive you experience each day. If something negative occurs, turn it around in your mind, reframing it into something positive. For example, let's say you were stuck in traffic. Why not assume the delay allowed you to avoid an accident. There is a benefit to focusing on what is good in your life as it gives your subconscious mind a directive to look for even more good. There is a "silver lining" to any cloudy circumstance. Look for it. As the book and film *The Secret* taught, "Focus on what you DO want."

Chapter Two

Gratitude

Principle: Thankfulness,

Tool: Affirmations

A teller at a bank drive up window was having difficulty with the glare of the sun, so he lowered the shade. The customers couldn't see him, but he could see them. As a woman drove up, the money drawer opened and she put her check in it for cashing. The drawer withdrew and soon it rolled out again with her cash in it. She took the money and stared at the window, where she, of course, could not see anyone. She said, "I know you're completely automated, but I want to thank you, anyway."

There is a part of us that wants to express gratitude. When we feel pleased with someone's gift or service to us, our natural response is to say, "thank you." Maybe it is deep within our consciousness, going way back to earlier times. The psalmist wrote,

"O come, let us sing unto the Lord…Let us come before his presence with thanksgiving, and make a joyful noise unto him…"

When our hearts are singing with gladness and joy, we want to give thanks. When you receive a gift, you automatically feel grateful. Gratitude is a result of the gift having been made. We feel so thankful that there really are not any words to express how we feel. That must have been the way William Shakespeare felt when he wrote these lines:

"I can no other answer make

Than thanks and thanks, and ever thanks."

- William Shakespeare

When have you felt that kind of gratitude? Take a moment and write down three times when you felt gratitude. There is always something we can be grateful for. And it is beneficial.

"Gratitude is one of the sweet shortcuts to finding peace of mind and happiness inside. No matter what's going on outside of us, there's always something we could be grateful for."

- Barry Neil Kaufman

When we train ourselves to express gratitude whenever we feel pleased and happy in what we have received, we can then reverse the process. When we give thanks, it can bring up the joy and gladness because the feeling and the expression have been intertwined in the mind. That's one reason giving thanks before a meal can benefit us. We feel pleased and that makes the body release endorphins, which helps us digest our food more beneficially.

Mark Victor Hansen, famous for co-authoring the *Chicken Soup for the Soul* series, notes,

"Say an original hand-holding grace over each meal. Expressing gratitude for the food we eat, uplifts the spirit – and even makes the meal taste better."

- Mark Vincent Hansen, *Dare to Win*

If you feel awkward saying grace, it is okay to simply give thanks silently. Get into a feeling of joy and gratitude for the food you are about to eat and for anything else that comes to your mind. Here is a prayer you could say aloud:

I AM GRATEFUL THAT GOD HAS PROVIDED THIS FOOD, WHICH NURTURES MY BODY AND KEEPS ME HEALTHY. AMEN.

Or if you are speaking for a group or your family, simply change it to:

WE ARE GRATEFUL THAT GOD HAS PROVIDED THIS FOOD, WHICH NURTURES US AND KEEPS US HEALTHY. AND SO IT IS.

When blessing your meal, keep it simple and you will be more likely to do it. Create your own prayer of thanksgiving that is easy to remember and uses words that are meaningful for you. By the way, do you know what you get if you cross a termite with a praying mantis? You get an insect that says grace before it eats your house.

When else should we express gratitude and for what?

"Give thanks even for those things which you do not see."

- Ernest Holmes

This leads us to a discussion of the most beneficial aspect of giving thanks. It causes you to be blessed with more that is good. As Eric Butterworth states,

"Thanksgiving is more than just an emotional response. It is a causative energy."

- Eric Butterworth, *Spiritual Economics*

Gratitude releases an energy that causes good to be created. When you are focusing on what you are thankful for, you are giving attention to it and attention sends energy. In the glossary of *The Science of Mind,* under "Thanksgiving," Holmes says,

"When we speak the words of thanksgiving to the God within knowing 'before they ask I will answer,' there is something in this attitude of thanksgiving that carries us beyond the field of doubt into one of perfect faith and acceptance…"

- Ernest Holmes, Glossary, *The Science of Mind*

There is a law of circulation that gives back to us whatever we have been focusing on. John Templeton, the famous investment guru, understands this principle and writes about it:

"Whatever you give your attention and belief to becomes your experience. So, focus your attention on the way you would like to see yourself. Give thanks for the realization that you are right now becoming that person. Give thanks for all of the abundance you're presently enjoying, and give thanks for the abundance of every good thing that's on its way to you. As you count your blessings and become increasingly aware of how truly blessed you are, you can begin to build an attitude of gratitude. Your life will be blessed in ways you never thought were possible."

- John Templeton, *Worldwide Laws of Life*

By giving thanks, you are blessing and praising your good, which attracts more good. I once read a story about a man who cursed practically everything. At work, he was told he had a bad attitude, so he blamed the boss for being overbearing. With his lousy attitude, he didn't do too well at work and since he was in sales, he didn't make much money. He got depressed about that and started drinking heavily. When he heard that he would get fired, he prayed, "God help me." Suddenly a great weight was lifted from his shoulders. He noticed a booklet that advised him to "praise anything that's bothering you." So he started seeing his problems as challenges and he blessed them as opportunities. He began to look for what good he could praise in his boss and others when he saw them behave in ways he appreciated. He expressed appreciation to customers. Soon he was promoted to store manager, got a terrific raise in salary and no longer had a desire to drink alcohol.

When we bless, praise or give thanks, we set into motion a powerful process. A mechanism in our minds goes to work searching for more of what we have blessed. We typically take so much for granted that we overlook what is right in our lives. By focusing on it, we increase our experience of the good and draw more to us.

It is sort of like a magnet. Henry Ward Becher said, "If one should give me a dish of sand and tell me there were particles of iron, I might look for them with my eyes and search for them with my clumsy fingers and be unable to detect them; but let me take a magnet and sweep though it and now would it draw to itself the almost invisible particles by the mere power of attraction.

"The unthankful heart, like my finger in the sand, discovers no mercies; but let the thankful heart sweep through the day and as the magnet finds the iron, so it will find, in every hour, some heavenly blessings. Only the iron in God's sand is gold!"

You might have noticed that you are already using gratitude since you are keeping track of your "wins." The same principle applies. You are using your "faith muscles" as Al Cohen describes it:

"Gratitude, like faith, is a muscle. The more you use it, the stronger it grows, and the more power you have to use it on your behalf. If you do not practice gratefulness, its benefaction will go unnoticed, and your capacity to draw on its gifts will be diminished. To be grateful is to find blessings in everything. This is the most powerful attitude to adopt, for there are blessings in everything."

- Alan Cohen, *I Had It All the Time*

"In all things give thanks."

- The Apostle Paul, I Thessalonians 5:18

Spiritual Tool – Affirmations

When we announce or proclaim what we intend to be thankful for in the future, we call it an *affirmation.* An affirmation is a brief statement declaring the real Truth of your being and how you are choosing for your good to show up in you life. For example, say,

I AM GRATEFUL I AM PROSPEROUS!

The power in affirmations is repetition. As part of your assignment for this chapter, I suggest you say an affirmation ten times and at ten different times of the day, for a total of one hundred affirmations per day. I AM GRATEFUL I AM PROSPEROUS is powerful and short enough for you to remember in accomplishing your assignment easily.

However, you may prefer other words. Also, there are times when you will want to use affirmations for other specific purposes such as I AM ALIVE, ALERT, AWAKE, ENTHUSIASTIC! or ONLY LOVE PREVAILS.

Don't make it difficult. Using affirmations is one of the simplest and yet powerful spiritual techniques available. The basic "rules" of writing affirmations:

1. Keep your affirmation brief so that you can remember it for frequent repetition..

2. Use words that are powerful and meaningful for you.

3. Use phrases that carry a punch. Invoking the I AM consciousness by using those two small words is very powerful.

4. Use first person words such as "I am," "I have" or "my" or

"mine."

5. Use the present tense, not past or future. If you declare, "I will be prosperous," the creative Mind will say "yes" to you being prosperous in the future, and as long as you keep saying it, the future will never arrive. Claim it now.

6. Affirm whatever is good for all. "I am now prosperous" does not exclude anyone else from prosperity and it is good for all for you to prosper. Wealthy people benefit so many others through charitable giving, purchases and providing jobs. Avoid affirming anything manipulative, such as "My boss appreciates my work." Say instead, "I feel appreciated for my work."

Once you have written your affirmation, there are many ways to use it. The most important elements are repetition and feeling. Write your affirmation fifty or one hundred times. Place post-it notes on your bathroom mirror, in your car, on your refrigerator, next to your computer and everywhere your eyes gaze. Try singing your affirmation over and over. Get into the feeling of the affirmation. Mean it when you say it. That is why I capitalized the affirmation I AM GRATEFUL I AM PROSPEROUS!

Assignments

1. Write down one good thing; a "win" that happens every day.

2. Spend at least four minutes in meditation daily.

3. Repeat a prosperity affirmation ten times at ten different times daily.

Chapter Three

Guiltless

Principle: No guilt,

Tool: Journaling

One of the major barriers to prosperity is feeling guilty. If people feel guilty, they will believe themselves to be unworthy; not deserving of life's blessings. Since belief creates our experiences of life, guilt leads to struggle and strife, limitation, lack and failure. If we felt guilty, we would find ways to sabotage our success. And we would be very creative about it.

I read of an Air Force Major who entered a Texas mental institution for the second time in 1959. He had tried to commit suicide twice, had been arrested for forgery and robbery, had been drinking heavily for years, and his marriage had fallen apart. What was the cause of all of these problems? Guilt. It seems that fifteen years earlier, he had been a model officer, promoted in his Air Force career regularly, and had lived a happy life. Then he flew the lead airplane over Hiroshima on the mission that ended World War II with the dropping of the Atomic bomb. He began having bad dreams and eventually punished himself by excessive drinking and the negative behaviors listed above. Guilt can be a powerful agent.

Most of us do not have such dramatic circumstances about which we might feel that guilty. Indeed, my experience has been that any guilt I have harbored has been well disguised. I once discovered that I had a twinge of guilt for reading a "Daily Guide" in *Science of Mind Magazine* for the wrong day. Somewhere along the way I had accepted a belief that reading the wrong page was bad; thus, I was guilty.

"A good man brings out good things from good treasures, and a bad man brings out bad things from bad treasures."

- Matthew 12:35

If we believe ourselves to be "bad," we will tend to bring out bad treasures; negative experiences. Many times we hid our negative emotions and attitudes from ourselves. We do not even realize those negative emotions about ourselves are there. We seem to have blind spots.

That term has its source in a physical reality. We do have blind spots in our physical vision. We do not actually see an entire 180 degree field in front of us. There is a "hole" or gap in our field of vision caused by a spot on the retina where there are no visual receptors in an area of about 1/16th of an inch in diameter. This is a tiny spot in your eye where the optic nerve and blood vessels enter the retina. Try this experiment. Cover you right eye and look at the circle on the right side of the next page. Keep staring at it as you get closer to the page and don't let your eyes shift. When your eyes are about twelve inches away from the page, the circle on the left will seem to disappear.

Your brain normally fills in the blind spot; usually our eyes shift and with both eyes in use, the blind spot is filled in. Notice that the circle on the left returns as your eye shifts.

There are also blind spots in our perception of ourselves. Rather than resulting from a physical circumstance like your eye, attitudes and belief systems cause these character blind spots. A person is "blind" to seeing one's own selfishness, egocentricity, or meanness because he or she does not want to believe him/herself to possess any of those qualities. Then, we *project* the characteristics onto someone else.

Fortunately, there is a way to discover what negative characteristics we possess that we are not seeing. We can look for characteristics that we see in others that we despise. If I have a lot of energy on someone else behaving a certain way, I can be sure I am projecting a little of myself onto him or her.

When we discover the truth, it sets us free, because we no longer operate with a false belief about someone else. We can take responsibility for our attitudes and personality characteristics and take action to change what we desire to change. We need to awaken to ourselves, then we can do something about it.

We all have made what we call mistakes. The Truth is that there are not mistakes; it is all perfect. The past was perfect because it led to the learning experience in the present. However, it we think we have made mistakes that are bad, or if we believe we have offended others, or if we think others have offended us, it is time for forgiveness work. If you can truly say and mean, "I am innocent of any wrongdoing, and everyone else is innocent," then you are "guiltless" already. If you believe you were wrong or wronged, however, it is time to forgive both yourself and the other.

Unforgiveness is heavy burden to carry; it saps our energy. It creates blockages in the flow of Life in our relationships, our bodies and our financial affairs. A Chinese proverb states,

"The one who pursues revenge should dig two graves."

A man took a forgiveness workshop and commented afterward, "I'm so glad I took this workshop on forgiveness because I used to hate my Uncle so much, I vowed I would never go to his funeral. Now, I'd be glad to!"

Forgiveness is an inside job. We do not necessarily need to verbally forgive someone or be forgiven by them in order for us to benefit from forgiveness. The bottom line is how you feel about yourself and others. Is there any residual resentment, anger or negativity of any kind? The place to work on your own negative emotions is right where the emotions are; within you.

Fortunately, that is exactly where the answer is found. That is where forgiveness lives – within you.- because God is the forgiving energy which is Love. It is not that God forgives. God doesn't need to forgive, because God has never perceived anything wrong about you. Contrary to popular opinion, God does not and will not judge you. You judge you.

Clara Barton was the founder of the American Red Cross. A friend of hers recalled a cruel thing that had previously happened. "Don't you remember the wrong that was done to you?"

"No," Clara replied, "I distinctly remember forgetting that.

Actually, you do not need to forget in order to forgive. In fact, by remembering the past, we can learn from experience. Also, you need not condone wrongdoing. Forgiving is not condoning. Forgiveness is not about being a martyr, either. We have not really forgiven if we harbor a feeling of self-sacrifice about the situation. Forgiveness is not done to be saintly or altruistic, either. You do it for your own sake.

"Be merciful just as your Father is merciful. Do not judge and you will not be judged. Do not condemn and you will not be condemned. Forgive and you be forgiven." - Luke 6:36-37

Forgiveness is a tool you can use to change your feelings and you are made of feelings, according to Terry Cole-Whittaker. She writes:

"Feelings are more than the function of life, *they are life itself.* They are the soul...The soul doesn't have feelings, it is feelings. Whatever feeling you have, that's what the soul is in that moment.

"Have the feeling of love and the soul is love.

"Have the feeling of fear and the soul is fear.

"Because this is so, you actually define yourself by the feelings you have. By the feelings you have you choose who you are, and by the feelings you have you also create your reality."

- Terry Cole-Whittaker,

The Inner Path From Where You Are To Where You Want To Be

So, let's do some activities to work with forgiveness. First make a list of anyone and everyone you think you need to forgive and who you think needs to forgive you. Write their names below.

Forgiveness List

Those who I think I need to forgive:

1._____

2._____

3._____

4._____

5._____

6._____

7._____
8._____
9._____
10._____

Those who I think need to forgive me:

1._____
2._____
3._____
4._____
5._____
6._____
7._____
8._____
9._____
10._____

Now let's work on these lists with a guided meditation. Have someone read the following meditation to you or record it for yourself.

Naturally when we work with forgiveness, we will feel joy when we let the blame go, so know that it's OK to express yourself with tears of joy, should they appear and you might want to have some tissue handy. Keep the book open to the place marked "Meditation Notes" to use following the meditation.

Meditation

Move into the meditation position that feels most comfortable for you. Close your eyes, and quiet your mind. Breathe in and follow your breath as you silently say "hum" to yourself. Breath out saying "sah." Do this several times……

Now see your breath as a bright golden or white light coming in and going back out again, swirling around you and within you……The light protects you through this meditation…..

Imagine that you have written the names of the people on your "Forgiveness List" on some stone tablets. You carved the names onto the heavy pieces of rock. Now, put the stone tablets in a large bag and drag it behind you as you begin a journey.

See yourself walking along an illuminated path. There doesn't seem to be any specific source of light, but everything is glowing. The air is fresh and you feel fully alive. The only thing that seems to hamper you is the weight of the bag you're dragging. You hear a voice within you assuring you and telling you to move forward on the path.

Eventually you come to a clearing with a brighter glow of light than you've ever seen before. The light is emanating from a large circular building. As you move closer, you notice the door is open and the light is actually coming from inside the building. It feels as if you are being beckoned to come in. You feel safe and protected. The place feels loving and secure.

You pull the bag with the heavy tablets as you climb the step and enter the building. Right in front of you there is an information counter and someone asks if you need assistance. You tell them you're here to work on forgiveness. You are told that you'll find

"The Center of Forgiveness" straight ahead. It's located in the very heart of the circular building. So, you move to the center noticing that there are rooms around the center marked "Wisdom Room," "Love Sanctuary," "Peace Pavilion," "Joy Room" and many others that you can visit some other time.

But now, you open the door to "The Forgiveness Center" which is radiant with a glow of light. You feel warmth and love here. No one is in the room except you right now. There are two chairs facing each other in the middle of the room. You move over by the chairs and take the stone tablets out of the bag, setting them on the floor. You sit down in one of the chairs and make your self comfortable. It's good to relax after the long journey carrying the heavy load. Soon it dawns on you what the other chair is for. You have a knowing that one by one, the people on your "forgiveness list" will join you in the room and sit in the other chair. The room is so filled with love, that you know this will be a wonderful experience.

When you're ready, see the first person on your list coming into the room and sitting in the chair. Look straight into his or her eyes with love and compassion. Perhaps nothing needs even be said for you both to feel forgiveness. Maybe you can sense the presence of the Christ within each of you...the Divine Self...the Buddha nature... the true Soul or Spirit. Or perhaps there are some things that need to be said. Let the words of forgiveness be shared.....

When you are complete with forgiveness, bring in someone else from your "Forgiveness List" and look in his/her eyes and let forgiveness happen with that one. Continue this process until everyone on your list has been forgiven or has forgiven you. You will have ten minutes of earth time to complete this process.

[Long pause]

Now, take one more minute to finish your forgiveness process with the last person.

[One minute pause]

Good. Have the last person leave the room and notice how light you feel and what a burden has been lifted from your shoulders. Glance at the stone tablets on the floor and you'll see that the names have disappeared. All you can see on the tablets are hearts carved beautifully in the stone.

As you rise from your chair, leave the stones where they are and leave the "Center of Forgiveness." You can return to this room should you ever need to forgive or be forgiven again. You'll remember how to get here. You leave the building but take the glow of light with you as you return along the path feeling light and joyful. Eventually you return to the place where you began this meditation.

Gradually begin to move your fingers and hands, your toes and feet. Stretch and gently open your eyes. Write your experience and your feelings in the space provided here.

Meditation Notes

_____
_____
_____
_____
_____
_____
_____
_____
_____
_____
_____
_____
_____
_____
_____
_____
_____
_____
_____
_____
_____
_____
_____
_____
_____

In forgiving yourself and others, you have unburdened your self; any old feelings of guilt or shame should now be lifted. If not, you might want to repeat the meditation until you feel totally free of negative emotions around needing to be forgiven or needing to forgive.

For now, we'll move on to this week's spiritual tool, which you actually already been using – journaling.

Spiritual tool - Journaling

This tool can be used in many ways. You might want to section off your journal for various purposes. Use a loose-leaf notebook, spiral notebook or any other book with plenty of blank pages, either lined or unlined, as you prefer. Mark sections for writing your "Wins," for notes following meditation time, for questions, quotations, insights, dreams and dream interpretations, affirmations, writing your feelings and "dialoging."

Hopefully these sections are self-explanatory, except for "dialoging" which we'll work with right now.

I learned to dialogue a number of years ago when I felt there were unresolved forgiveness issues about my father. I had wonderful parents and a great childhood. However, my Dad, like many fathers, didn't make it a practice to show physical affection with his children. His words didn't necessarily express his love either. So I didn't feel as loved as I now know I really was. It's just that Dad showed his love by being a good provider, sharing knowledge, showing interest and taking the family to movies, outings and vacations. But I seemed to need more.

So I dialogued. I wrote the dialogue like a script for a play or a movie (without stage directions, however). This is sort of how it looked:

Don: Dad I'd like to talk to you about something.

Dad: Sure, Don boy. What is it?

Don: Well, Dad, I just want to ask you about why you never hugged me or showed me love.

Dad: Hugged you? Uh, I guess I never thought about it. Men just didn't do that much.

Don: Did you love me?

Dad: Of course I did. What do you think? Sure.

And the conversation continued until I felt complete and felt that I had actually had a conversation with my father and really knew that he did love me. It's amazing how real the conversation seemed and how easily I could know what words he would use.

Part of your assignment this week will be to create your own dialogue with someone. It could be about an old issue or something that comes up during the week. Experiment with it and see what happens. Create your journal and use it. You'll grow in your spiritual development.

Assignments

1. Re-read the chapter in order to review and absorb the concept of "Guiltless."

2. Write down at least one good thing that happens each day - a "win."

3. Increase your meditation time to six minutes this week. Spend at least six minutes in meditation every day.

4. Repeat your Prosperity Affirmation ten times at ten different times each day.

5. Finally, create and write in your Journal. Write a dialogue and be prepared to share your success with another person.

Chapter Four

Goodness

Principle: Prosperity and Money are Good

Tool: Positive Prayer

Introduction

This chapter is about "Goodness." We'll explore attitudes you might be holding that are not conducive to prosperity – attitudes that wealth, money and prosperity are evil in some way.

Prosperity Principle #4 – "Goodness"

> "God is Spirit. Spirit is substance and substance is supply. This is the keynote to a realization of the more abundant life, to the demonstration of success in financial matters. It is right that we should be successful, for otherwise the Spirit is not expressed. The Divine cannot lack for anything, and we should not lack for anything that makes life worth while here on Earth."
>
> - Ernest Holmes, *Science of Mind* 262.3

Everything that makes life worthwhile here on Earth comes from

God. That makes it all good. So abundance is good, wealth is good, prosperity is good, success is good and money is good.

God promised Moses a land of milk and honey. Symbolically, that means wealth. Moses didn't live to see the land, however, and it was left to Joshua to cross over. It's not that Moses hadn't reached the place to cross. In truth, he sent twelve spies over to check things out. They spent forty days over there and brought back a bunch of grapes so big they had to carry it on a pole between two men. And they brought some pomegranates and figs. "Indeed the land flows with milk and honey and this is the fruit of it," they reported.

But they also said that the people in this land were well fortified, strong and there were giants in the land. Ten of the twelve said, "Don't go." Joshua and Caleb urged them to cross over. The people feared a negative outcome and took the advice of the ten. They were looking at the negative, not what was good. They were run by fear, not drawn by a higher vision and faith in the basic goodness of it all.

Of course, when they focused on the negative, the law of cause and effect responded and the result was that they spent their lives in the wilderness and died there - all except for Caleb and Joshua. Joshua maintained a mental equivalent of knowing he could conquer the land. When they finally did go into Canaan, he accomplished it in only three days.

In *Homesick for Heaven*, Walter Starcke asserts, "The question isn't whether we are finite or infinite, perfect or imperfect, mortal or immortal, but whether we identify ourselves with limitation and the body or with infinity and freedom."

What are you identifying with in your life? Are you seeing what's right? Or are you focused on your problems and limitations? Do you acknowledge what is working or what isn't?

Two men were traveling the land searching for prosperity and as they traveled, they came to a stream that seemed to pose a problem for them. They discussed what they should do. One argued that they should swim for it. They could use their strength to get to the other side. The other noticed the rapid current and advised they stop and listen for Divine Guidance. Impatient, the first man said, "I'm swimming for it." He jumped into the water only to be carried downstream and submerged under the turbulence in the river. The second man found a comfortable spot to sit down by the stream to meditate. As he relaxed, his eyes fell on something glittering beneath the surface of the water. He looked more closely, and there he saw layers of gold in the shallow part of the stream. The prosperity for which the men searched was right there all the time. One man saw the problem; the other saw the gold.

Religion has focused on the negative aspects of the material world. Behind this negativity is a spiritual truth, but it has become distorted. The spiritual truth is that the spiritual realm is so much more vastly important than the material world in the hierarchy of the universe, so that when we live our lives only looking outside of ourselves for success and money, we miss the richer, more meaningful aspects of life. Thus the scriptures state,

"For the love of money is the root of all evil."

- I Timothy 6:10

Notice that it is not money that's the root of all evil, but the *love* of money. Since everything is made of God stuff, money is really God's energy, so it cannot be bad. But religions are correct to point out that the material world is not where it's at. Loving money or any *thing* is a mistake because you're focusing on outer world effects rather than the inner causation of Spirit.

"But seek first the kingdom of God and his righteousness, and all these things shall be added to you."

- Matthew 6:33

If we really knew who we were, we wouldn't need to seek the kingdom. We're in it already. Life is good. God has given us every good thing and it is ours to enjoy. As it says in the twenty-third Psalm,

"Surely goodness and mercy shall follow me all the days of my life; and I shall dwell in the house of the Lord for ever."

- Psalm 23:6

A minister was giving a lesson to a group of children on the 23rd Psalm. He noticed that one of the little boys seemed disquieted by the phrase "Surely, goodness and mercy shall follow me all the days of my life..."

"What's wrong with that, Johnny?" the pastor asked. "Well," answered Johnny, "I understand about having goodness and mercy, for God is good. But I'm not sure I'd like Shirley following me around all the time."

As we discovered in the previous chapter, you are "Guiltless." You are basically good. Goodness is your nature.

A well known speaker started off his seminar by holding up a $20 bill. In the room of 200, he asked, Who would like this $20 bill? Hands started going up. He said, I am going to give this $20 to one of you but first, let me do this. He proceeded to crumple the dollar bill up.

He then asked, Who still wants it? Still the hands were up in the air. Well, he replied What if I do this?

And he dropped it on the ground and started to grind it into the floor with his shoe. He picked it up, now crumpled and dirty. Now who still wants it? Still the hands went into the air.

"My friends, you have all learned a very valuable lesson. No matter what I did to the money, you still wanted it because it did not decrease in value. It was still worth $20. Many times in our lives, we are dropped, crumpled, and ground into the dirt by the decisions we make and the circumstances that come our way.

"We feel as though we are worthless. But no matter what has happened or what will happen, you will never lose your value: dirty or clean crumpled or finely creased, you are still priceless to those who love you. The worth of our lives comes not in what we do or who we know, but by WHO WE ARE. You are special - Don't EVER forget it."

I wish whomever sent that story to me over the internet would have identified the speaker, so I could thank him for a great illustration of two valid points: You are special and of value, and so is money. Both have basic goodness. They are worthy of our respect.

In her top selling book, *The 9 Steps to Financial Freedom,* Suze Orman says,

"Respect for your money and respect for yourself are linked. Building one builds the other."

She suggests an exercise of taking out your wallet and seeing how your bills are organized – ones mixed in with tens – fives with twenties. Are they all facing the same way? Are they stuffed in so you have to unravel them? She explains that keeping your bills neat and in order serves as a constant reminder of the respect that you and your money deserve. Rev. Noel McGinnis once shared with me how he organizes the money in his wallet. He puts the larger denominations in front so that he sees the higher amounts first, subconsciously telling his mind he is prosperous. Stop reading right now while you take out your billfold or purse and organize your money.

Other symptoms of disrespect are constantly paying late fees by forgetting to make payments or not returning purchases that you made and didn't really want. Other indications of disrespect are overspending frivolously, paying high interest, and misuse of credit cards.

Remember the goodness of money. It's prosperity principle number four. Be good to yourself by honoring money. Before we move on to this week's prosperity tool, take a moment to reflect on the concept of "Goodness."

Prosperity Tool – Positive Prayer

Next let's explore this chapter's prosperity tool – positive prayer. There are many names for positive prayer including affirmative prayer, spiritual mind treatment, prayer treatment, spiritual treatment or mental treatment.

Positive prayer differs from traditional prayers of supplication because they are based on the assumption that God has already provided our good and doesn't need to do anything. We are the ones who need to do something, and that is, we need to accept the bountiful good God provides. So we affirm our good. We take a positive approach.

The dictionary defines prayer as: "1. A reverent petition made to a deity or other object of worship. 2. The act of making such a petition. 3. Any act of communion with God, such as confession, praise, or thanksgiving. 4. A specially worded form used in addressing God. 5. A fervent request." Positive prayer would include "communion with God," "thanksgiving," "a specially worded form used in addressing God," and "fervent."

Positive prayer is prayer that works.

Perhaps you have heard of the Religious Science minister, who had a parrot that would only say, "Let's pray." A friend who was a Unity minister had a parrot whose vocabulary consisted only of "Let's kiss.' The two ministers decided that if they put the two together, maybe they would be inspired to learn other phrases. So the Religious Science minister took his parrot over to the Unity minister's house and thy put the two birds in a cage together. Pretty soon the Unity minister's parrot said, "Let's kiss.' The other parrot replied, "Thank God, my prayers have been answered."

Jesus promised…

> "Everything that you will ask in prayer, believing, you will receive."

- Matthew 21:22

And…

> "Anything you pray for and ask, believe that you will receive it, and it will be done for you."

- Mark 11:24

Notice that there are two actions we must take: asking and believing we will receive it. God does the rest. If you don't make your request known, don't expect it to show up. And if you don't believe you will receive, you won't.

"Let is be done to you according to your belief."

- Matthew 8:13

So how do we change our belief about a condition that we have seen with our senses? Our mind has accepted the validity of what we have perceived. How do we convince it otherwise? Obviously, we must give the mind a new picture, a new reality. That can be done in a number of ways. We can imagine it to be different, we can visualize a new reality, we can act as if the new reality is already so. In Richard Bach's *Jonathon Livingston Seagull*, an older gull tells Jonathon:

> "To fly as fast as thought, to anywhere that is, you must begin by knowing that you have already arrived…"

We must feel as if we are already there and then we are. Positive prayer is one way to "fly" there.

I have seen so many prayers answered and have had uncounted answers to prayer myself. So I am convinced of the effectiveness of Positive prayer. Perhaps one of the most dramatic examples of answered prayer occurred when my family was young. I was working at a radio station in Pomona, California. We had attended a few New Thought churches for about four years and when we moved to California, began going to the Unity Church in Pomona. But I hadn't yet learned how to really pray effectively.

The flu was going around and nearly all of my family caught it. I was home in bed with it. My third daughter, Jennifer was only about nine months old at the time and it hit her hard. When she worsened, my wife called the Doctor's office. Our regular one was out of town. She was told to take Jennifer to the hospital. When she got there, Jennifer began convulsing from dehydration. She was given Valium to stop the convulsions, but had an abnormal reaction to it and stopped breathing. The nurses were out of the room at the time, but fortunately my wife was there to call for help immediately. They rushed in and got her out of the room while working to stabilize Jen.

When my wife inquired about the progress, she spoke to the Doctor who had been called in – Dr. Doubtful. True to his name, when my wife asked if her baby would live, he said he didn't know. And if she did live, he didn't know how much brain damage might have occurred from lack of oxygen. Some other women in the visitor's room consoled my wife and she called me to have me come to the hospital. I got out of my sick bed and rushed over there. By this time, they had Jennifer hooked up to intravenous liquids. The tubes entered one side of her head and she looked disfigured. One side of her mouth seemed to be drooping and she was unconscious.

Eventually we realized there was nothing more for us to do but pray, so we went to the Unity Church. They contacted the minister, who said she would pray from where she was, and we sat in the sanctuary in meditation and prayer for about two hours.

When we returned to the hospital, Jennifer was wide-awake, the tubes had been removed, he face was normal and she said, "Daddy!" I hugged and kissed her and thanked God for the miracle. She has never suffered any ill effects from the incident. (She does have a very unique personality, however.) Prayer works.

Essentially, there are three elements of positive prayer that make it effective.

1. Deity – God is.

2. Oneness – I am.

3. Naming your intention – I claim.

You could actually narrow this formula down to two ingredients: spiritual awareness and conscious direction. Recognition and oneness are the needed ingredients of spiritual awareness and naming your intention is giving conscious direction in your prayer. The founder of the Science of Mind taught three steps of "Spiritual Mind Treatment." Later he acknowledged that two more elements are present in a Treatment: Thanksgiving and Release. So the Religious Science movement (Centers for Spiritual Living) now teaches a five step formula:

1.. Recognition

2. Unification

3. Realization

4. Thanksgiving

5. Release

The late Rev. Stretton Smith, who created the "4T Prosperity Program", taught a three-column prayer:

1. Recognizing God in column one.

2. Identifying with the "I am" in column two.

3. Affirming your goal in column three.

Other New Thought teachers have taught seven and even twelve steps of spiritual treatment or affirmative prayer.

My desire is to keep it a simple as possible, while including the necessary ingredients in working with prayer for your prosperity. By using the Deity, Oneness, Naming formula, you'll be able to remember it easily, because it spells out my name D-O-N.

The first ingredient to Positive prayer is "Deity." No matter what name for the Creator and Sustainer of the universe may be, you know there is something that is a Force for good. In this first step of prayer, recognize this Power and the characteristics of the Deity that apply to your particular prayer request. If your prayer is for money or prosperity, you might acknowledge the characteristic of "abundance." If you are praying for good health, some of the God-like characteristics are "life," "perfection," and "wholeness." If you want improved relationships, include "love." For guidance, include "wisdom." You get the idea. Include the attributes or characteristics of the Deity that are appropriate for your intention.

Here's an example of using this first ingredient in a positive prayer for prosperity:

    D. "God is the source of the infinite, bountiful abundance of the universe."

For now, you may wish to keep each step or ingredient of your prayer brief. Later you can expand to embellish the feeling of it more fully.

The second ingredient of positive prayer is "Oneness." This is where you identify with your own spiritual nature. For now, until you learn the ingredients completely, use positive prayer for yourself. Later you can pray for others using the same formula, but in this second step, you would also acknowledge the "oneness" of the other person. We have already discussed your "goodness" due to the Truth of your being that you are spiritual in nature. This ingredient of the prayer is done simply to remind yourself of this Truth. Since you cannot be separated from God, but only forget who you are, include "oneness" to realign yourself using words similar to this:

    O. "I am one with the source of all supply and prosperity."

The third ingredient is "Naming." Basically, this is an affirmation, but you might make it longer to "feel" the Truth of it and form a clear image in your mind of the new reality you are claiming. Name it and claim it. Claim it in the present, not tomorrow. Be specific about *what* you are claiming, but not *how* God will create it. Name and claim anything that is good for you and harms no one else. Say something like this:

> N. "I accept increased income, a new home, wonderful car, order and balance in my financial affairs, more than enough money to pay for my wonderful lifestyle and plenty left over to share and to spare. I am grateful I am prosperous!"

Please note that you should be feeling joyous and thankful at this point, but you don't have to actually voice your gratitude. Simply check to see that you are feeling happy and complete about what you've claimed. In concluding your positive prayer, you might like to finalize it with an "Amen" which means "sealed in faithfulness" or "And so it is."

Now it's your turn. Write your own positive prayer in the space provided. Then, share your treatment with someone.

The purpose of my positive prayer:
_____
_____
_____
_____

"Deity" – God is:

_____
_____
_____
_____
_____

"Oneness" – I am:

_____
_____
_____
_____
_____
_____
_____
_____

"Naming" – I claim:

_____

_____
_____
_____
_____
_____
_____
_____
_____

You may use the positive prayer you have written or write a new one for the week or one each day as part of your assignments this week.

Assignment

1. At least one time this week re-read the material in order to review and absorb the concept of "Goodness."

2. Write down at least one win that happened each day.

3. Increase your meditation time to eight minutes this week. Spend at least eight minutes in meditation daily.

4. Repeat your Prosperity Affirmation ten times at ten different times each day.

5. Write in your Journal about your feelings when using positive prayer.

6. Read aloud or make up a positive prayer to say at least once a day.

Chapter Five

"Gladness"

Principle: Importance of being happy in your work;

having enthusiasm

Tool: Mind mapping

Introduction

This chapter is about "Gladness." We need to be happy in our work or daily life activities and experience enthusiasm for all that we do.

Prosperity Principle #5 – "Gladness"

Our fifth prosperity principle is based on a simple psychological truth. When we are happy, fulfilled and positive, our lives run more smoothly and we prosper. But when we are unhappy, sad, angry or negative, nothing seems to go right. When it rains it pours.

Most likely no one would choose to be unhappy and experience negative circumstances. So I am not presenting any startling news here. The question is, how can I be happy and positive in the midst of limitation, lack, chaos, confusion, disharmony, upset and all the negative conditions of life that I may be facing?

The first step, of course, is to be aware of the negativity. That seems obvious. Yet, I am constantly amazed at the number of people who are apparently oblivious to what kind of energy they are entertaining and how negative they are being. Somehow we have convinced ourselves that the outer world determines our inner states of mind. The opposite is actually the Truth. You determine your feelings and attitudes about the circumstances of life. Furthermore, you play a part in actually creating those circumstances. Most of the time, we create unconsciously, thereby surprising ourselves when the events appear.

In her book, *Building Your Field of Dreams*, Rev. Mary Manin Morrissey notes,

> "When you hold an intention, you direct energy. If you do not consciously intend your dream to become reality, you unconsciously intend that something else will take form. Your very nature directs energy."

We begin by becoming aware of what we are experiencing. Based on what we see manifesting in our lives, we can deduce what we must have been holding in our minds that would show up in this way. This is not done to beat ourselves up. It is done so that we can see that our thoughts create our circumstances of life. This can be empowering as we realize that we are in the driver's seat. We are steering the vehicle of our lives. If you are steering, you can turn to the right or the left to determine what direction you want to go. If I delude myself into thinking someone else is in charge, I will feel powerless and victimized.

"There are no victims in the universe, only creators."

- God in *Conversations with God by* Neale Donald Walsch

Having determined who is responsible for the way our lives will be, we can then move to the next step and begin to change our attitudes and thoughts. That is where gladness comes in. It is my contention that we have the option of choosing gladness or sadness. I'm not criticizing sadness. Psychologically, there are times when it is important to mourn a seeming loss. If we have chosen an emotion, it is best that we express it in some harmless way. Don't deny what you have chosen. But once you get it out, get over it and choose again.

The place where negativity most affects our level of prosperity is in the workplace. If you are unhappy in the very work that supplies your income, it's pretty obvious you'll be struggling with prosperity.

If you are retired or don't work at a job, your "workplace" is wherever you conduct the life activities in which you are engaged. The same principles apply.

Ralph Waldo Emerson advised us to be totally zealous about our work:

"No matter what your work, let it be your own. No matter what your occupation, let what you are doing be organic. Let it be in your bones. In this way you will open the door by which the affluence of heaven and earth shall stream into you."

Is your vocation in your bones? Are you happy in your job? Can you whistle while you work? There was a boss who requested his employee to stop whistling while he worked. The employee replied, "Oh, I'm not working, sir, I'm just whistling."

A study of 3,381 workers revealed that 42% felt "used up" at the end of the day and 40% felt tired in the morning when going to work. In addition people are working more hours today than they were twenty years ago. Across the country, 50,000 people quit their jobs each day. Many others quit their jobs but keep going to work. Another poll showed that nearly 85% of the workers in the United States said they could work harder on the job. More than half claimed they could double their effectiveness, if they wanted to. And a huge 95% do not enjoy their work!

Deepak Chopra, M.D. has noted that more people die of heart attacks at 9 a.m. on Monday mornings than any other time of the week.

No wonder you can find tongue-in-cheek announcements such as this one on an employee bulletin board:

> "IN CASE OF FIRE, FLEE THE BUILDING WITH THE SAME RECKLESS ABANDON THAT OCCURS EACH DAY AT QUITTING TIME."

Staying in a job that you dislike while complaining about it is not going to prosper you. So you have two choices. You can quit your job or you can change your attitude. If you quit your job, be sure you "heal" any false beliefs or you will carry them to the next job, only to re-experience them until you resolve them.

Quoting Eric Butterworth in *Life is for Living,*

> "Many of the problems that we fret over are bound to us by the hold we have upon them. It is the old story of the nettle: as long as a man holds it in his hand it will continue to sting. He has to let go."

Usually fear stands in the way of quitting a job. That fear is based on a belief in limitation; that there are not enough jobs to go around; that the Universe won't provide for you if you don't have that salary. You can probably see the self-deception here intellectually, but it's the underlying belief at the emotional level that's operating. If your belief system says there is limitation, you had better not just quit your job stepping out in faith, because the faith you have is faith that you will be unemployed and penniless. It is done to you as you believe. It's important to recognize what is in your belief system about it.

When I graduated from ministerial school, I was terminated from my radio job that very month. The station was going to be sold to owners who planned to offer Spanish language programming only. My talents didn't include speaking Spanish. In this case, my belief system said I should be a minister of a church. But I looked for another radio job in the meantime. You probably won't be surprised to hear that I couldn't seem to be hired. Nothing worked out. At one point a station was going to fire an announcer to hire me, but because I believed I should be a minister, and because I believed it wouldn't be fair to adversely affect that announcer's life, I turned it down. I finally accepted a temporary overnight shift until my perfect church position came through.

So, did I create being terminated in the first place? Certainly I played my part. Throughout my ministerial schooling, I was becoming less and less interested in broadcasting. Subliminally, I'm sure my attitude was shouting, "I'm outta here!" Not so subtle was my tendency to show up at the last minute before my air-shift and leave as soon after it as possible.

Fortunately, my over-riding attitude throughout this experience was that of faith. I knew Divine Spirit was preparing my perfect position in the ministry. That enabled me to do well at my job and experience "gladness" while doing it temporarily.

If you are reasonably happy with your life activity right now, but wish to increase your prosperity, you might try increasing your level of "gladness" by moving into a state of enthusiasm about it.

"Enthusiasm" is defined as "rapturous interest or excitement, ardent fondness or eagerness; zeal. Archaic: ecstasy arising from supposed possession by a god." The root word "theos" is the Greek word meaning "God." So, when we are enthusiastic, we are embodying a God like characteristic. And that's good for us.

On page 440 of *The Science of Mind,* Holmes wrote,

> "When (a man) gives himself with enthusiasm to any legitimate purpose, losing himself in the thing which he is doing, he becomes normal and happy."

Another writer in the field of the Science of Mind and Spirit, Arthur Thomas wrote in his book, *Abundance is your Right,*

> "(Enthusiasm)…is a part of your resident nature. It can be generated and become a strengthening part of your life."

If enthusiasm is part of your nature, you should be expressing "gladness" constantly. What's in the way? What are the barriers to your natural expression of enthusiasm? Is your work boring and tedious? Are you unchallenged? Are you discouraged by slow progress? Do you seem to have to play too many politics? Do you believe your workplace to be a negative environment? Write down what barriers you can identify that have inhibited your enthusiasm in your work. On the following page, make a note identifying the barriers.

The apparent barriers to my joy in the workplace:

_____
_____
_____
_____
_____
_____
_____
_____
_____
_____

Behind every barrier is a belief that holds it in place. An example from my own career follows. When I was in college, I worked part-time for a local radio station. I sold advertising airtime and had the opportunity to record my first real life commercials for some of my clients. I had a ball as I eagerly learned about the business and gave it my all. A friend, who helped me get the job, decided to leave. He quit in anger accusing the owners of being greedy. Eventually, my belief in their greed caused me to become discouraged and unhappy. I quit after only a few months. Looking back on it, I can now see that these owners were taking a big risk and had invested all their resources in the radio station. They weren't really greedy, just running scared. But I had let my belief that it was not OK to work for greedy people make me unhappy.

Next, identify your beliefs that may be holding the barriers you have identified in place.

Beliefs that may be holding barriers in place:

_____
_____
_____
_____
_____
_____
_____
_____
_____
_____
_____
_____

Now, share with a friend or a group such as a prosperity circle what you have written and then brainstorm together to come up with possible alternative beliefs to "reframe" the negative beliefs. In the example I gave, the beliefs I identified were that the owners were greedy and that it was not OK for me to work for greedy people. Reframing those beliefs, I could say, "The owners were fearful and perhaps I could serve them by selling more airtime." Even if I still believed in their greed, I could make it OK to work for them with something like, "I am learning about the broadcasting business and being paid for it, so I am generously rewarded."

On the next page, write your "reframed" beliefs:

_____
_____
_____
_____
_____
_____
_____
_____
_____
_____
_____
_____
_____
_____

Once you change your beliefs, remain vigilant to be sure the old beliefs don't sneak back into your thinking. Use positive prayer and affirmations to adjust your attitude.

Many times our beliefs create bosses or co-workers who we can label as "wrong." They validate our beliefs by acting negatively. It is important to our well-being and happiness that we return only love to everyone no matter what they may be doing to us. As Emmet Fox points out in *Power through Constructive Thinking,*

> "Nothing can come into your experience unless it first enters your mentality, and nothing can enter your mentality unless it there finds something like itself to which it can attach itself. As long as your heart is really

clear of ill will, you are perfectly safe. On the other hand, the use of the power of thought in hostility to others could only result in very severe suffering and punishment for yourself. According to your belief is it done unto you. To think evil of Tom, Dick or Harry, is to think evil; and to think evil, *ipso facto*, is to call it down upon yourself."

One useful technique to deal with seemingly difficult people is to throw them a "love ball." In fact, we can do that right now. Relax and bring to mind that seemingly negative person. See him or her acting in a way you dislike. Then, form a "love ball" by gathering up energy between your hands. Form the ball out of light. Make it as small as a baseball or as large as you can hold. Put love into it and form it with care and nurturing. See the love ball as pure light. When you are satisfied that the love ball is filled with unconditional love, toss it at the person. Hit him or her right in the face with it. See the love splashing all over the person. Notice his or her reaction. The bosses and co-workers we've showered with light and love won't know what hit them.

Is there someone else who comes to mind that could use a "love ball?" Go ahead and see them in front of you. Form another love ball of light and love. And when you're ready throw it on that person and let the love cover and fill him or her.

You can repeat this simple but effective process on your own with as many people as you like. Some of your wins this coming week will undoubtedly be about the amazing changes in attitude of these persons.

Teach yourself to be loving and accepting of everyone and everything, you and your life circumstances included. Be like the woman who saw that her house was partially blown away by a tornado. Others were saying, "What a tragedy." But as she emerged from the storm cellar she commented, "We were going to move anyway. Now I won't have to pack a thing."

"Be joyful always."

Find joy and enthusiasm in all areas of your life, especially your work. Kahlil Gibran advises:

> "If you cannot work with love but only with distaste, then you should quit your job and go sit at the temple and beg alms from those who work with joy."

Prosperity Tool – Mind Mapping

I would like to share a tool with you that brings me a lot of joy. Mind mapping is a way to use more of your brain and tap a higher percentage of your mind than normal. Mind mapping can enhance creativity so that you make certain tedious tasks fun. It can be used for note taking, creative writing, increasing mental retention, outlining, speech making, brainstorming and any activity in which you want to tap both sides of your brain.

The left side of the brain in most people is the mental side that deals with technical data, linear thinking, numbers, math, dates, history, logic and rational thinking. The right side is the creative side, which responds to music, art, colors, patterns, beauty, dance, poetry, emotion, feelings and humor. Both sides of the brain are important. Ideally there is a balance. We all know some people who are more adept at using one side or another. Engineers, mathematicians, statisticians, analysts, scientists, computer technicians, historians and accountants tend to be right brain dominated. Painters, sculptors, musicians, singers, actors, dancers, poets and inventors tend to be left brain dominated. Left-brained people use their intellect; right-brained people use their intuition. Everyone has both sides. And everyone can learn to use more of one side or the other, if they so desire.

Separating the two sides of the brain is the Corpus Callosum, the function of which is to integrate and communicate between the two sides.

Mind mapping is designed to enhance that process, thereby providing access to a greater percentage of the brain's capabilities and tapping in to more of the genius mind that resides within and around us. When you use more brainpower and mind power, you can achieve more, accomplish much and reap the benefits of unlimited abundance and fulfillment in your life.

Mind mapping uses colors, patterns and pictures to align with the right brain. It uses key words, numbers and order to align with the left brain.

Use a large sheet of unlined paper. Place the topic of the mind map in the center of the paper and circle it. Branch out from the circle with straight lines on which you write key words or short phrases. Let's call the line that comes out from the circle the primary line. Draw a line out from the primary line with a descriptive word or phrase related to the word or phrase on the primary line. Then continue to branch out with other related thoughts out from those lines. This is somewhat similar to the way we used to diagram sentences in school, but you aren't concerned about parts of the sentences and you need not include all the words.

Use a different color for each branch that comes off the circle. I like to start in the upper right hand corner of the circle (about 2 o'clock) and work my way around the center in a clockwise manner. However, you can start wherever you like.

Draw little pictures, stars, happy faces, geometric patterns or whatever your right brain inspires you to draw. Connect related thoughts with dotted lines and arrows if you like. Enclose each branch cluster with a balloon or cloud shape to finish it off.

On the following page, I've drawn an example of a mind map about mind mapping.

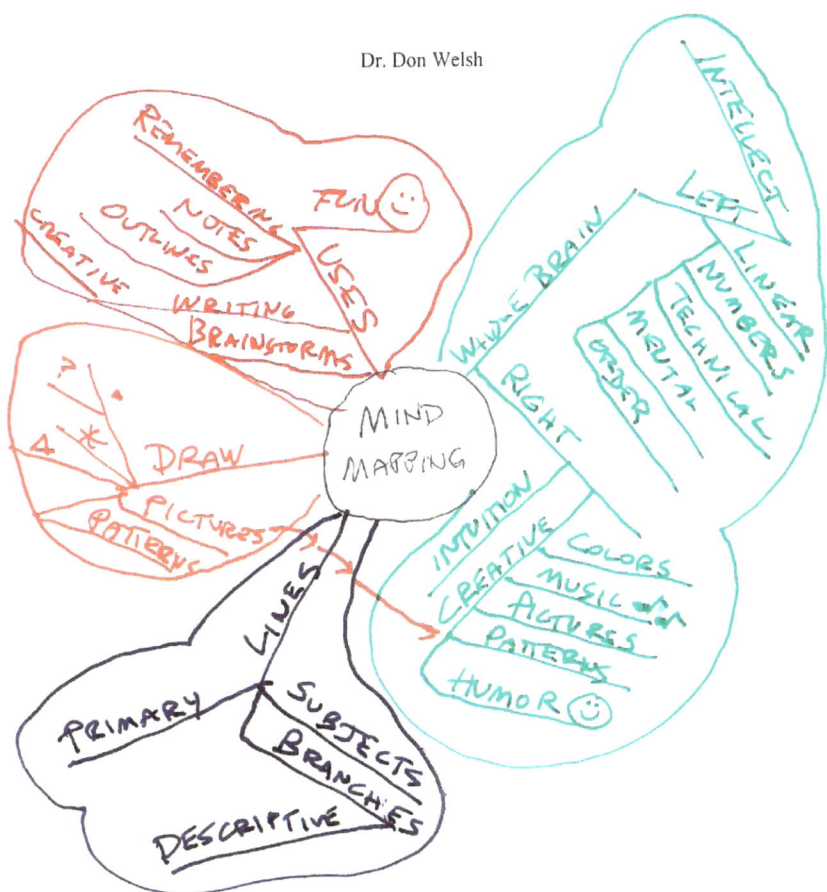

Now it's your turn. Draw a mind map on a separate piece of unlined paper. Turn the paper sideways, so the longer side is horizontal in front of you. Use colored pens if available. In the center of the page, print the topic "Creating Joy" and begin to make a mind map showing how you intend to increase the joy in your job and/or life activities. Then explain your mind map to a another person.

I'm sure you'll have fun with mind mapping and no doubt you'll find ways to apply it in many areas of your life.

Assignments:

1. Read the material on "Gladness."

2. Write down one "win" each day.

3. Spend at least ten minutes in meditation each day.

4. Repeat your prosperity affirmation ten times at ten times daily.

5. Try mind mapping in your journal.

6. Read aloud or make up a positive prayer to say at least once a day.

7. Create a Mind map about what makes you happy.

Class #6

"Guidance"

Principle: Listening to the Inner Genius for Divine Direction

Tool: Visioning

Prosperity Principle #6 – "Guidance"

Because you are a spiritual being, you are always immersed in the Intelligence and Wisdom of the Universe. Whatever guidance you need is always available for you. Unfortunately, most people believe that they are separate from God and therefore separated from the Infinite Omniscient Mind. Omniscient means all-knowing and certainly Spirit knows all. But as Terry Cole-Whittaker says in *How to Have More in a Have-Not World,*

> "...The vast majority of the population of this earth, at least 95%, live as victims or potential victims of forces they believe are outside of themselves."

A car was involved in an accident. As one might expect, a large crowd gathered. A newspaper reporter, anxious to get his story, pushed and struggled to get near the car. Being a clever sort, he started shouting loudly, "Let me through! Let me through please! I am the son of the victim."

The crowd made way for him. Lying in front of the car was a donkey.

Don't claim to be a victim! You are not at the affect of anything outside of yourself. You are in charge and empowered because you are a son or daughter of God. The Father-Mother Spirit indwells you and provides everything you require for a happy, healthy, successful, fulfilling, love-filled prosperous life. And that includes Divine Guidance. As Ernest Holmes wrote,

> "The answer to every question is within man, because man is within Spirit, and spirit is an Indivisible Whole."
>
> - Science of Mind 442.3

You are always being guided. Your intuition provides ideas and insights constantly. The question is "Are you always listening?" Somehow we tend to get caught up in the activities of the outer world and fail to listen.

A mother and her 3-year-old daughter were riding in a car when suddenly the little girl put her head on her mother's chest and began to listen. "What are you doing?" mom asked.

"I'm listening for Jesus in your heart," was the reply.

"Well what do you hear?"

The innocent child looked up with the satisfied look of discovery in her eyes and said, "Sounds like he's making coffee to me!"

Whether you think of the Christ-like nature to be in your heart, or the Divine Intelligence to be in you mind, Spirit will guide you if you will listen.

Wouldn't it be wonderful to always know that you're making the right decisions? That you will always be in the right place at the right time doing what's right for you? Let's go through a typical person's day and see where it would benefit him or her.

Let's call her Anna. She awakens early, refreshed and alive, writes in her journal about the insights she's received in her dreams. She takes the time to meditate and gets clarity about the direction for her day. When she eats breakfast and all her meals, her intuition reveals which foods will best serve her. Anna drives to her workplace avoiding traffic by following inner guidance and arriving alert and happy, anticipating a successful day. She knows exactly what to say to everyone with whom she does business, thereby attracting amazing deals and successful transactions. Anna was guided to this vocation by meditating and visioning. She is fulfilled by her work and amply rewarded for her talents. She empowers others by intuitively knowing what will support them. By the end of the day, Anna has the same ease in driving home that she did that morning as she automatically takes the best route. She stops to make a purchase and checks her inner guidance to get the best value. She spends wisely. In the evening she enjoys activities that bring her delight as she uses the time for optimum benefit, having listened for Spirit's direction. And of course, she attends a Spiritual Prosperity Class and gains great meaning and understanding.

So what is Anna's secret? Maybe she learned it from scripture.

> "Be still and know…"

> - Psalm 46:10

When we're focusing our attention out here in the world, we can miss the wisdom that Divine Mind has for us. Ram Dass states the obvious:

> "The quieter you become, the more you can hear."

Later, we'll learn about the spiritual tool called "visioning" that helps us gain clarity about everything in our lives. You'll find it to be a useful tool.

There are other techniques for gaining guidance. One idea came from Alan Cohen in a workshop I attended once. He said to flip a coin to decide! First you determine what decision "heads" represents and what "tails" means. Flip the coin and when you see the result, notice your first reaction. Are you pleased or disappointed? If you're pleased, it was the right decision. If you're disappointed, go with the opposite choice. If you're willing to keep it simple and trust in this process, it will always work for you. Want guidance? Flip a coin!

Another technique is to watch for signs. I was literally guided by a sign one time when I needed guidance about my career path. Actually, my guidance involved two techniques. First, I meditated with a piece of paper in front of me and pen in hand. I affirmed that Spirit would provide the ideas I needed. Sure enough, as I meditated, ideas came to me about a variety of possibilities about what to do regarding my work. I was closing an advertising business that hadn't succeeded and desired direction for what was next. As ideas came to me, I noted them with a word or two on the paper in front of me without breaking my meditative state. In a few minutes I had a list of ten or so possibilities. So then I asked that Spirit guide my pen in marking a number by each idea. Without really looking at the paper, and while remaining in meditation, I put the numbers 1 through 10 on the paper. I knew that #1 would represent the highest choice for my work and the others would carry less weight in making my decision.

As I opened my eyes, #1 was placed nearest "DJ." I couldn't believe it! I had been a DJ and/or announcer for nearly twenty years and had moved beyond it by becoming an advertising agency owner. I assumed my system hadn't worked. So I went for a walk in the rural mountain neighborhood in which I lived. I had taken walks before along the highway and up a mountain side. As I set out, I noticed a mailbox two doors down that I'm sure had always been there, but I hadn't seen the initials on it before. You guessed it, they said, "D – J!" I continued on my walk and ended up underneath some tall Fir trees contemplating the guidance. I decided to make a call or two and at least investigate the idea.

I reached a former boss, who said he had a weekend position open. "Ah," I thought, "that's it. Just a part-time job on the side while something else shows up." I took the job and two week's later the mid-day slot opened up and it was offered to me. The pay would be such that when combined with another part-time job at a Science of Mind Church, handling PR, I would make more money than I had ever made before. It helped finance my ministerial training.

When the Church job ended, I again desired guidance. One night, I read an article in *Success Magazine* about a company in Texas that was doing well creating recordings for businesses to play over their phone systems while people were on "hold." I thought, "that's interesting," threw the magazine in the wastebasket and went to bed. I did a Spiritual Mind Treatment (positive prayer) before going to sleep that I would be guided in my job situation. The moment I awakened in the morning, I realized that article in the magazine had been the answer all along. I retrieved it, re-read the article, shared it with a potential partner and within a week had formed a start-up company in Silicon Valley called "Information On Hold, Inc." It generated cash flow very soon and provided more income to the family than what I'd been making before.

Notice that I needed to do more than just get the guidance. I had to take action.

> "If they obey and serve Him, they will spend their days in prosperity and their years in pleasure."
>
> - Job 36:11

Obey the intuitive voice within and you are serving Spirit by doing what's good for you and good for all. You automatically prosper when you follow through on Divine Wisdom's desires for you.

Another technique for receiving guidance is to connect with a visualized image of Wisdom showing up as an inner Guide. While it seems that a wise being is appearing, it is really a projection of your own Higher Self that you are revealing to yourself. Let me guide you through a meditation for guidance using this technique. First, determine what you would like guidance about. Write down a question to ask your Higher Self. Form the question in such a way that could be answered with a "yes" or "no."

As you prepare for this guided meditation, have some paper available to make notes afterwards. Either record and play back the meditation or have someone read it to you.

Make yourself comfortable, in whatever meditation position you prefer. Gently lower your eyelids, to avoid visual distractions. You may want to place your feet flat on the floor, uncross arms and legs, sit with your back straight and your head held high, letting Energy flow through your body easily and freely.

Relax every part of your body, while letting your mind remain conscious and alert. Mentally inventory your body to check that all areas are comfortable and relaxed. Begin with your toes and work your way up to the top of your head and if you find any discomfort, send energy to that area by visualizing it immersed in light. Choose whatever color of light that will soothe the area immediately and bring it into alignment with your natural state of wholeness and perfection. Take a moment to survey, relax and align your body now…..

Good. Feeling relaxed but alert, focus your attention now on a path you've been on before. It's that path that leads to a large illumined circular building. The path is luminescent. The air is fresh and clear. You move easily toward the building, dazzled by the brilliance of the light emanating from it. You walk up the steps and move through the doors. The Light is coming from within the building. There's the information desk again. You ask for direction to the "Wisdom Room." You are told that you'll find it near "The Center of Forgiveness" which you visited before. You go straight ahead toward the center of the circular building. You notice the other rooms nearby marked "Love Sanctuary," "Peace Pavilion," "Joy Room," and "The Center of Forgiveness." You enter the door marked "Wisdom Room," and as you enter, the Light is intense and uplifting. The air is crisp but the temperature is perfect. You hear the soft voices of a choir of some sort in the background. Your mind is alert and you sense that you will learn something valuable here today. You eagerly move to a chair facing a large screen, like a movie screen. As you wait there, you remember the question you would like answered – the guidance you would like to receive.

With the question in mind, you notice that the lights begin to dim. Suddenly a wise being enters the room, glowing with light and love. This wise one comes up to you and looks deeply into your eyes. You see great wisdom here. You feel the love and caring emanating from this master. You decide to ask your question, knowing that this being knows what your highest and best good would be regarding this matter. Go ahead and talk to your guide right now.

Let the guide respond and provide you with whatever wisdom is appropriate for you to know. Nothing is withheld. Your mind is filled with illumination. The inner guide reveals the answer.

To confirm further that you are truly receiving valid guidance, the wise one presses a button and a movie starts up on the screen. It shows how your answer will play out in your life… You are getting further clarification regarding your guidance. Let the movie continue until you know for sure that you have received the wisdom you requested.

As it concludes now, you commit its contents to memory. Converse with your guide one last time and say whatever will complete this experience for you.

The guide now bids you farewell as you leave the "Wisdom Room" and return to the front of the building, going out the door, down the steps and back along the path. Filled with your new insights, you bounce along with a skip in your step and a lightness about you.

Begin to return to this time and space now remembering everything about this inner journey and prepared to make some notes about what guidance you have received. So return your awareness to the room now. Begin to move your toes and fingers, roll your head and gently open your eyes. Write whatever notes are appropriate on the paper in front of you.

Prosperity Tool - Visioning

Next we'll explore this week's prosperity tool, visioning. First, let's make it very clear that *visioning* is not *visualization.* In visualization, we conjure up an image in our minds that we would like to experience. In visioning, we let the images or ideas simply come without outlining the content or expressing our opinion or preferences about the vision.

Dr. Michael Beckwith of the Agape Center of Truth in Culver City, California, has used visioning effectively in building his church of thousands of members. He defined visioning in an interview in *Science of Mind Magazine* a few years ago as follows:

> "Visioning is a process by which we train ourselves to be able to hear, feel, see, and catch God's plan for our life or for any

particular project we're working on. An organic process that has evolved for me as I grow spiritually, it is based on the idea that we're not here to tell God what to do or to ask God for things but to absolutely be available for what God is already doing, to open ourselves up to catch what's already happening."

- Science of Mind Magazine, December, 1996, p.38

But the idea of seeing God's vision didn't originate with Dr. Beckwith. Ernest Holmes is quoted in the same issue of the magazine, saying,

> "It is necessary...to find higher visions and broader vistas of thought if we are to transcend our previous experience."

Ibid. p.7

So how do we "vision?" What is the process of "visioning?"

The first requirement is to clear your mind of any preconceived ideas or notions of what you *should* receive. Let go of all judgment, opinions or preferences. Enter into a visioning session with an open mind. Be an open vessel for Spirit to fill. The assumption is made that your conscious mind doesn't know everything. But it is your conscious mind that needs to become aware of more of Ultimate Reality. The Mind of the Universe holds a grander vista of all that is than the conscious mind of humankind can hold. Yet you are interconnected with Spirit and therefore have immediate and direct connection with the Source. You can tune in to your Divinity and know more than you thought you knew.

Second, enter the visioning process knowing that God is totally for you and never against you. The Infinite is pro-love, pro-health, pro-prosperity, pro-joy and pro-wisdom. There is nothing the Creator would withhold from you.

Third, enter into a meditative state in whatever way is most useful for you.

Next, keep asking "What is the highest idea in the Mind of God? What is the Divine direction? What is God's vision?" and similar questions.

Remember what comes to you and accept it without editing or judging. I received guidance to get a van for the vehicle my Church leased for me. My logical, conscious mind wanted to argue with the idea, questioning the cost and practicality. My thinking mind gave me some reasons to have the van, but that part of the process wasn't visioning, it was rationalizing. I told myself the Church could use my van instead of our big bus and save money. I acted on my guidance and went to a local car dealer. There to my surprise, was one of the congregants of my Church. He was co-owner of the dealership and offered to help in service to the community and my Church. I leased a seven-passenger mini-van and drove it home. The next Sunday the bus transported TEN passengers. It became clear to me that Spirit wanted me to have the van, but had no part in the use of it to replace the bus. I have had opportunities to carry a number of passengers and just loved the van. Spirit knew I would and wanted me to enjoy it. I didn't need to rationalize it with my conscious mind.

Before moving from Miami to Lancaster, California, I visioned for guidance about the timing. My meditations had indicated a move would be appropriate. I listened for instructions and received guidance that I would hear something at the annual Asilomar Conference that summer, where I was to be an "emcee" that year. Sure enough, I learned that the ministers of two west coast churches planning retirement. They were Camarillo, California and the Antelope Valley Church in Lancaster.

I continued to vision regarding when to put our Townhouse on the market to sell it in preparation for moving. Guidance told us, "November first." We interviewed real estate agents and felt good about a man and woman who worked together. We told them we would put the Townhouse on the market November first. Coincidentally, that was the day the Antelope Valley Church of Religious Science in Lancaster advertised an opening for a new minister. My resume was the first they received. Our Townhouse sold in only five weeks for the amount we needed to cover our investment. We had lived there less than two years, so it was remarkable that we got our money out of such a short-term investment. Furthermore there were identical units for sale for thousands of dollars less.

We delayed the close of escrow as long as possible since we didn't know for sure where we would be moving. But when I spoke at the AV Church on the first Sunday of January, I knew it was the place to which Spirit was guiding me. We returned for a second visit at the end of February and I was hired. We closed escrow March 8th. Due to a contract agreement, I gave sixty days notice to the Miami church and we moved to an apartment for two months. But had we not followed Divine guidance about when to sell, we might not have gotten our investment back. After we moved, the market took a downturn of several thousand dollars. I served the AV Church for more than ten years, so apparently it was a good match.

Visioning can be used for any situation, large or small. In about 1975, I used visioning without knowing what it was called when purchasing a TV set. I asked for guidance and based the purchase on inner guidance. Amazingly that television set lasted twenty years without any major repair! Spirit knew.

So, visioning can be very practical or very mystical. You can use it on any decision or question and you will receive an answer. God is there for you.

Let's have a brief visioning session right now. Determine

something you would like guidance about and write it down.

Now prepare yourself in the same way you would for meditation.

Relax your body from the tip of your toes to the top of your head. See yourself breathing in Light and releasing any shadows of negativity you may have been holding.

Survey your body and send Light wherever more comfort could be expressed. Relax.

Now ask for the highest idea in the mind of God to be revealed relative to your desired guidance. What is Spirit's intention? What is God's vision about this question? Listen and receive the guidance. Be still. What does God desire? Receive the guidance easily and clearly. Know that you know the answer.

Ideas come to you. Images emerge in your mind. Be receptive to the wisdom. Accept the vision whether by seeing it, hearing it or feeling it. Let yourself be guided.

Let your memory hold on to the guidance you have received as you gradually open your eyes and return your focus to the outer world. When you're ready, write about your visioning experience and the guidance you received.

In group visioning for a common purpose, it's important to share what you received as different participants may have unique insights, which combine with others to provide a more complete picture of the whole intention.

Assignments

1. Read the material, "Guidance."

2. Write one "win" each day.

3. Meditate at least twelve minutes daily listening for guidance.

4. Repeat your prosperity affirmation 100 times daily.

5. Write in your journal with questions for and answers from the Universe.

6. Read or say a positive prayer at least once a day.

7. As either part of your meditation time or as a separate activity, listen for guidance daily using Visioning techniques.

8. Make notes of your visioning using mind mapping.

Class #7

"Goals"

Principle: Intentions – Delineation of Desires - Expectations

Tool: Goal Setting

Introduction

Welcome to your next principle of *The Mystical Ten*. I know that through the use of the principles and tools in this book, Inner Wisdom has guided you and made your way clear to accept a higher level of livingness, success and prosperity. This chapter is about "Goals." As we are clear about our highest desires, expectations and intentions, our focus on our goals results in the manifestation of our good through the Creative Process.

Prosperity Principle #7 – "Goals"

In a sense, we're always working on goals. Sometimes those goals are consciously affirmative, such as "I choose to be wealthy," and sometimes they're unconscious and negative. For example, how often are you saying, "I am lacking" or a similar phrase expressing limitation? This following list of "don'ts" reveals areas in which people unconsciously affirm lack:

Don't save for a rainy day (or you'll get plenty of them).

Don't defer living now (by always meeting tomorrow's requirements instead of today's).

Don't worry about failing.

Don't look at money as evil.

Don't affirm that you're on a fixed income.

Don't limit the possible sources of income.

Don't dwell on negativity or even on lists of "don'ts" like this one!

We must constantly be vigilant of the attitudes we harbor. If we have a lack consciousness, we'll work against ourselves and experience, loss, lack or limitation. There's a saying from Jesus that seems unfair, but when you think about it from the standpoint of consciousness, it makes sense:

> "For to him who has, it shall be given, and it shall increase to him; but he who has not, even that which he has shall be taken from him."

- Matthew 25:29

Ernest Holmes advised:

"Each should train [oneself] – and do so consciously – to conceive of [oneself] as a success…All thoughts of failure or depression must be erased from the mentality, and positive thought of achievement should take their place."

- *The Science of Mind* 450.5-451.1

Who doesn't have a desire for success, achievement greater goodness of some kind? Catherine Ponder writes in *Open your Mind to Prosperity,*

"Desire is God trying to give you greater good."

A goal is an intention to experience something you desire. It's natural to have goals and the Universe supports those who delineate their desires. God wants you to live abundantly. Again quoting Holmes:

"Know that the greater abundance of every good thing which you are bringing out in your life, the more perfectly you are satisfying the Divine Urge within you. ANYTHING YOU CAN DREAM OF is not too great for you to undertake, if it hurts no man and brings happiness and good into your life."

- *The Science of Mind* 288.2

I saved a newspaper article about a family that won the California lottery a number of years ago. They had been down and out with $35,000 worth of debts and no money to pay the rent and utilities. The husband had been out of work. The wife is quoted as saying, "We knew something had to happen, but we didn't expect this." Something had to happen. That is an affirmation. And it worked.

Is it all just luck? I think not. Our experiences of life are the result of our beliefs and actions. Golf pro Gary Player said, "The harder you work, the luckier you get."

Someone has said that if you're waiting for your ship to come in, you should check to see if you have given it sailing orders. The universe rearranges itself according our picture of reality. Try giving yourself sailing orders. Repeat these affirmations, taken from the workbook by Dr. Mary Jaeger and Kathy Juline, *You are the One:*

>"I always have a great deal of money."
>
>"I spend money wisely."
>
>"I am financially successful."
>
>"I have money to buy what I want."
>
>"I am always financially secure."
>
>"I have a savings account."

"I joyfully release money."

"Everything I need is provided."

"I manage money well."

"I love and bless money."

Of course, prosperity amounts to more than just money, but money's a big part of it, isn't it? We each have a slightly different idea of what would be prosperity for us. Wealth means different things to different people. H. L. Mencken defined wealth as "Any income that is at least $100 more a year than the income of one's wife's sister's husband."

No matter what your goals may be, the odds are on your side that you will achieve them. Why? Because there is a tendency for good to happen and the Universe supports you in accepting your good. But that might not be true of your friends and acquaintances. In his book, DO IT: *Let's Get Off Our Buts,* Peter McWilliams says,

"Keep the trolls away from your goals."

He points out that there are people who can't stand to see other people succeed; they're the trolls. He compares them to crabs. It seems that crabs could not be caught and eaten if they didn't have a certain inborn trait. When a cage is lowered into the water with an opening at the top of it and bait inside, a crab will climb in and start eating. Pretty soon another comes along and another. Soon the bait is gone, but the crabs won't crawl out. They easily could, but they don't. Even after the bait is long gone, more crabs will join the "feeding frenzy" and climb in the cage. If one of the crabs even tries to crawl out, the others pull it back down and even pull its claws off if it persists.

The book suggests that you notice who's in the cage with you. If you know your family and friends will support your dreams, go ahead and share them. If you're unsure of friends, try telling the dream to them saying it's someone else's dream. If they say, "that's great; good for them," feel free to share your goals. But if they say how ridiculous it is or respond in any negative way, don't share your goal until you've reached it.

Why does goal setting work? When you have clarity about your intentions, you are more focused, and when you are focused, there is a movement of energy in the direction you desire. If there is no negativity or contrary belief between where you are right now and where you intend to be, the energy will move instantly to create the manifestation of your goal. If there is any barrier in the way, focusing on the goal will rapidly bring the barrier to the surface so that you can deal with it. The barrier won't stand up to the Truth of the Light, and you'll be ready to accept your good.

Let's use a hypothetical situation as an example. Let's say Ruth, a housewife, desires to work outside the home in a fulfilling, high paying position. She writes down her goal. "I am joyfully employed in a fulfilling, high paying job right now." Notice that she has written her goal as an affirmation, which is a very effective technique. She repeats her affirmation several times. She shares her desire with her husband and he's supportive. Their children are old enough that Ruth doesn't need to be at home all day. But the very first day that Ruth began affirming her goal, her children had special activities and needs that demanded her attention. Ruth handled everything but realized that had she been working, she wouldn't have been there for her kids. She begins to feel guilty and thinks of herself as selfish for wanting to work outside the home.

Ruth's desire could have been squelched right then and there. But Ruth recognized the pattern of guilt that surfaced and journaled about her feelings. She came to the realize that she tended to give too much and that it would actually empower her family more at that time in their lives for them to take on more responsibility for their own needs. Ruth had a family meeting and explained her desires to the kids. They understood and promised to do whatever they could to take care of themselves. She continued affirming her goal.

She lined up three job interviews within twenty-four hours. As she was getting ready to go to the first appointment, affirming, "I am joyfully employed in a fulfilling, high paying job right now," fear crept in to her mind. She thought to herself, "What am I doing? Here I am nearing middle age and I expect to get a job?" She quickly realized that the barrier of a false belief in an age limitation had appeared combined with an old pattern of feeling "not good enough."

She took a few minutes to give herself a positive prayer including worthiness and the Truth that any age is the perfect age to begin a career. She convinced her mind of this and dismissed the fear as False-Evidence-Appearing-Real. Each time a negative belief or barrier came up, she handled it and kept on affirming. All three jobs were offered to her and she chose the one that fit her desires in every way.

Don't let any false beliefs or limited thinking get in the way of attaining your goals. Be prepared to deal with any barriers that may surface once you announce your intentions.

Since this week's prosperity principle and prosperity tool are the same, we'll move directly into discussing the tool of goal setting.

Prosperity Tool - "Goal Setting"

In order to set goals that are in alignment with your highest desires, let's begin with becoming aware of your purpose for living this life. Why are you here?

I've meditated and visioned on my purpose in life and discovered that I am here to love. I am on the planet to express the love that is my true nature. Now in order to be loving, there seemed to be some principles and ideas that I needed to learn. So a secondary purpose is to learn.

Keeping these ideas in mind, I can then formulate goals that will fulfill my purpose. I can begin by asking myself what I would like to do to express love. Here are some possible primary goals for me:

1. I learn all life's lessons gently and easily.

2. I express unconditional love for all people.

3. I love and accept myself unconditionally.

4. I accept and give all that is good.

5. I am in the flow of infinite abundance.

6. I inspire myself and others to be all that we are meant to be.

7. My body serves me well as a healthy temple of the Living God.

Each of these goals could lead to other goals, which more specifically affirm precise ways in which the higher goals are fulfilled. For example, within goal number seven above, there are numerous secondary goals I could affirm such as:

1. My body maintains vitality, balance and wholeness with an ideal weight and shape.

2. My heart beats strongly to the rhythm of life.

3. There is a free flow of Divine Energy in every part of my body.

Within the category of the flow of infinite abundance, I might have more specific goals such as "I am paid handsomely for the talents I share as a teacher, healer, minister and writer." If you use a specific amount in your affirmation, be sure to change it when you've reached it. As it says in New Design for Living,

> "Once our (income) goal is reached we need to be sure to establish another, or else the first goal becomes a limiting factor on any future accomplishment."
>
> - Ernest Holmes and Willis Kinnear, *A New Design for Living*

Now I have given some of my goals, but you need your own. Don't set your goals by what other people think is important, because you're the only one who knows what's best for you.

Pause now and write what you feel your life purpose is and follow it with some goals that match your purpose. You may either use the form below or mind map your goals.

MY PURPOSE

_____
_____
_____
_____
_____
_____
_____
_____
_____

PRIMARY GOALS

_____
_____
_____
_____
_____
_____
_____
_____
_____
_____
_____
_____
_____
_____

SECONDARY GOALS (within primary goals)

I choose this secondary goal to work with:

_____
_____
_____
_____

Next, get ready for a guided meditation for realizing your goal listed above. Have someone read to you or record and playback the meditation script. Set every thing aside and make yourself comfortable.

Assume your favorite meditation position and focus on your breathing. Relax. Let go of any distractions by taking an inventory of your body to make sure it's comfortable. Fill your entire body with Light. Let it flow around you and within you, relaxing you from the top of your head to the tip of your toes. Say to yourself "I am relaxed."

Remember the goal that you chose to work on. Now imagine that you are going to make a short movie that shows a scene of your life with this goal already accomplished. You are the Director. So, first select a setting. Where will this scene take place? Select whatever actors and actresses you'll need to be in the scene. You can either choose someone to play your part or you can be in your film. Have the actresses and actors visit the wardrobe department to select the right clothes or costuming for the scene and then they can go to make-up so they'll look just right.

Prepare the location however you would like it to be. Make sure that there's perfect lighting and camera placement. Bring the actors and actresses into the scene. They've studied their lines and are ready to perform. Now you're ready. You say, "Lights, camera, action" and the scene begins. Watch to make sure it's perfect and if it's not, yell "cut" and start over. All the cameras are rolling to catch the action from all angles. See the scene showing your life with your goal accomplished. Good.

Now take the film into the editing room and choose the camera angles you prefer. Make sure everything is perfect. Delete parts. Add music or sound effects. Build the scene the way you want it.

When you're ready, take the film to the viewing room. Everyone that you want to be there is there to watch your masterpiece. The projectionist starts the film. The audience is pleased and so are you. It's perfect. They give you a standing ovation at the end.

You tell your assistant that distribution can now send the film to theaters everywhere. Your scene is a reality and you are a success. The whole world cheers you on. Congratulations.

Hold on to a euphoric feeling of joy and gladness as you gently bring your attention back to the room. Begin to move about and gently open you eyes. Share your experience with someone about your movie and how it made you feel.

Goal setting is an important part of achieving your desires. Conscious use of this tool will propel you forward in accomplishing all your dreams and fulfilling your grandest idea of your life.

Assignments:

1. Re-read "Goals."

2. Write one "win" daily.

3. Meditate at least fourteen minutes daily.

4. Repeat your prosperity affirmation 100 times daily.

5. Write in your journal regarding your feelings about your goals.

6. Read or say a positive prayer at least once a day.

7. Listen for guidance through "visioning" at least once this week.

8. Mind map or list goals in the areas of health, wealth, relationships, lifestyle, spiritual growth and any other category that you choose.

Class #8

"Growth"

Principle: Expansion

Tool: Visualization

Introduction

Welcome to the eighth principle of *The Mystical Ten*. I know that you have defined and affirmed your goals and you're on your way to greater success and prosperity. Now we move on to "Growth." The Universe is always expanding, so expansion is a natural tendency. It's also natural for us to want to grow spiritually, mentally, emotionally and financially.

Prosperity Principle #8 – "Growth"

One commonly accepted theory about the origin of the universe is that there was a "Big Bang" and everything in the material world came into existence and evolved into what we see today. Scientists can measure distances between planets and other celestial bodies and have detected a very slow increase in the space between galaxies, stars, suns and moons. Theory has it that ever since the "Big Bang" everything has been moving out from the center of the bang and continues to do so today. That means there is no end to expansion. We live in an unlimited universe.

Just to get a concept of how unlimited everything is, imagine this. Our sun could contain one million planets the size of Earth. The Sun will continue to exist for billions of years. There are 500 million suns in our galaxy. The average galaxy contains 100 billion stars and there are one hundred million galaxies in known space with new stars forming all the time. It is an expanding galaxy in an expanding universe that doesn't no anything about limitation or lack. Think of how many pine needles there are on a single tree or how many leaves on a deciduous tree. Or, how about counting the number of grains of sand on beaches and in deserts and the number of drops of water in the ocean.

If expansion is the way things are, then growth is a given as well. It is the norm for growth to take place. Plants and trees are constantly growing and especially my lawn.

Even mountains can grow. I read of a mountain that grows about two inches every ten thousand years. Slowly, to be sure, but it is growing.

So, it's not surprising that there's something within us that moves us to want to grow. Humans mature emotionally and psychologically, expand their knowledge and become aware of more of their spiritual nature. We desire to be all we are meant to be. Maxwell Maltz, author of the 1970 classic bestseller *Psychocybernetics* said,

"You can find the Sun within yourself if you will only look."

Another writer calling himself "FM2030," talked about this "liberated rich" in his book published about two decades ago, *Are You a Transhuman?* He thinks the liberated rich are the forerunners of the rest of us and that his description of the liberated rich describes the way most of us will be in the future. He identified the characteristics of the liberated rich as people who can afford to have high values and "high tech." They rarely have to compete for anything, seldom rush, rarely express stress, only do work that they love at their own pace in their own way and have compatible collaborators. They have the resources and time to give generously to the world, are always *teleconnected*. They fly in helicopters for short treks and in supersonic jets for long hauls. The *translive* in a global environment, have many attractive liftoff and landing pads at apartments in cities, houses in the country, hotels, resorts, and on cruise ships. They live with a psychology of abundance.

How can we expand and grow to be all that we're meant to be? Since we are already perfect spiritual beings and all of the God qualities live as each of us, the way to expand is to awaken to the truth of our being – to be enlightened. Walter Russell was such a man. In the book, *The Man Who Tapped the Secrets of the Universe,* the author, Glenn Clark, wrote about this remarkable man who learned to be a writer, mathematician, musician, sculptor, artist, architect and philosopher. He truly tapped the Inner Higher Self and was all he was meant to be. Russell said,

> "God took me up into a high mountain of inspiration and intense ecstasy. A brilliant flash like lightning severed my

bodily sensation from my consciousness and I found myself freed from my body and wholly in the Mind universe of Light, which is God…. And the secrets of the universe were unfolded to me in their great simplicity as the doors to the Light opened fully to my consciousness…Thus knowing the static Light of God, and the two dynamic lights of His thinking, and the electric processes by means of which His thinking is recorded in 'matter' I at once had the key to all the sciences, mathematics, chemistry, astronomy and mechanics, likewise all the underlying principles of creation…"

I believe an important part of awakening to our true potential involves releasing any energy we are holding in the body, mind and emotions from old hurts and pains. If we can be here now, we can focus the mental, emotional and spiritual energy to achieve amazing results.

Another way to be all that we can be is to examine our belief system and change it when appropriate. In his book, *You'll See It When You Believe It,* Wayne Dyer states,

> If you believe strongly in scarcity, think about it regularly, and make it the focus of your conversations, I am quite certain that you see a great deal of it in your life. On the other hand, if you believe in happiness and abundance, think only about them, it is a very good bet you are seeing what you believe."

I saved an old newspaper article about a single mother. In 1986 she was living with her daughter in their car. By 1989, she owned her own cleaning business employing seven people. The shift started with her declaration "This is never going to happen to me again." She worked day and night as a full-time bookkeeper and began cleaning houses. She took a class called "The Finance Course" and learned about keeping your word, integrity, and to get rid of the excuses. She also learned about what she called "the big picture," one's ideal work, home and family life. If you go after "the big picture," present needs are taken care of. Strength of determination was a big part of this woman's success.

There were two thoroughbred horses discussing an upcoming race. One said, "I've *got* to win!"

"Why? It's only money for your owner," queried the other horse.

"Well, the boss said if I won, I'd get thirty extra bales of hay. I've gotta' win."

The other's response was "Thirty bales! Hay! That ain't money!"

Whatever we do to transform ourselves, it won't be difficult if we choose to keep it simple and let our path be easy. Take it one step at a time and let your consciousness expand steadily and smoothly.

When Thomas Edison came up with an invention for Western

Union Corporation, they offered him $100,000. But he couldn't grasp such a sum and it was a huge sum in those days. He told them, "The money is safer with you," and he made a deal for them to pay him $6,000 per year for about 17 years. Take it easy. One day at a time.

Specifically focusing on how to financially grow and expand, remember this simple truth. I learned it from the *Financial Freedom* class created by Rev, Lloyd Strom, and Rev. Marcia Sutton, Ph.D. They pointed out this principle:

When there is order and balance, expansion naturally occurs.

Let me repeat that and say it slightly differently, because it is extremely important. When you have order and balance in your financial affairs, expansion occurs automatically.

Balance has to do with income at least as large as the outgo. That's why we'll be looking at budgeting in the next chapter.

Order means keeping track of where you stand financially. It involves keeping records and knowing how much money you have in your checking account, among other things. I believe order also involves having our mental household in order. If we are carrying around a lot of negative memories about money, finances or our personal worth, they act as barriers to the natural expression of prosperity in our lives. Order and balance involve paying attention to your finances and our consciousness. Remember, where your attention goes, the energy flows.

In her book, *Open your Eyes to Prosperity,* Catherine Ponder tells the story of a businessman who succeeded even in economically depressed times. No matter what happened to others around him, he always prospered. People would comment, "Every thing he touches turns to gold." He revealed his secret saying, "Business is wonderful because there's gold dust in the air..." He would actually see gold dust in the air everywhere.

That's similar to saying that expansion is natural. Establish order and balance and remove any barriers to wealth's normal manifestation and you too will be saying, "There's gold dust in the air."

Nuerolinguistic Programming provides us with a technique to remove barrier and establish mental order about prosperity. NLP, as it's called, deals with our psychological conditioning which is perpetuated by our own habitual ways of thinking and feeling. "Nuero" has to do with the nervous system "linguistic" with how we language things for ourselves. NLP techniques help us to tell ourselves something empowering in place of negative patterns in our minds.

You can actually take a negative memory, see it on the movie screen of your mind, and shrink it by visualizing the scene as being smaller. Then you can focus on a positive memory and make it bigger in your imagination. Shrink your problems; enlarge your joys. NLP was the source of a guided visualization I have practiced and called "The Joy Shift." So when we move into the section on this week's prosperity tool of visualization, I'll provide you with a "Joy Shift."

Prosperity Tool - Visualization

Visualization is a very powerful technique to employ the inner resources of the mind. Athletes, actors and artists are using it regularly these days. Many studies have proven the effectiveness of visualization, such as one where basketball players were divided into groups and tested on their abilities to make baskets from the "free throw" line. One group actually practiced shooting free throws. Another group only visualized. And a third group both practiced and visualized. The results were that the group that practiced and visualized were able to sink some 9 out of 10 free throws. But amazingly, the group that only visualized did nearly as well as the group that actually practiced.

Football players visualize successful plays. Bowlers visualize knocking down all the pins. Pianists can visualize a perfect concert. In 1958 a man name Liu Chi Kung placed second to Van Cliburn in Tchaikovsky competition. A year later he was imprisoned during the Revolution in China. He was held for seven years and wasn't able to practice on the piano. But soon after his release, he went back on tour and played better than ever. Everyone wondered how he could do it without any chance to practice for seven years. Liu said, "I practiced every day. I rehearsed every piece I had ever played, note by note, in my mind." He visualized rehearsing on the piano. And it worked.

We are actually using visualization all the time. The moment someone suggests, "Let's go out for Mexican food," your mind conjures up an image of your favorite Mexican food and possibly even the restaurant that serves it. Depending on your reaction to the image in your mind, you'll say "yes" or "no" to the idea.

You just used your imaging ability to picture the scene I just told you about. That's the same faculty of the mind that you use for visualization. Let's use it for the "Joy Shift" I mentioned.

First, think of a situation in your life that you would like to change or experience differently right now. When I first tried this exercise, I was having a problem with water seeping into the basement family room of a house we lived in at the time. When I would think of the problem, I would feel upset and frustrated. Pick whatever situation you would like to work with. Determine what it is you'll work on transforming.

When you have a situation in mind that you would like to experience differently, close you eyes and relax. Have someone read this meditation to you.

Breathe deeply following the breath in and out. Relax your whole body. Feel the Light of Pure Spirit filling you from the tip of your toes to the top of your head and swirling around you and moving through you. Be the Light. Relax.

Remember the situation you have chosen to experience differently. Just stay with it, even though you would like to forget it right now. Good.

Now I invite you to remember a peak experience…a time when you were elated. You were successful and joyful. People praised you and you felt fulfilled. Take a moment to remember this highlight in your life. Feel the joy of the moment.

Now, hold on to that feeling of joy as you return your mental attention to the negative situation you chose to work on. Just keep the feeling of the peak experience and bring the joy into the negative scene. Go back and forth, seeing the negative and swooping back to the joyful situation. You are bringing the joy from the exhilarating scene into the memory of the scene you want to transform. Continue going back and forth between the two. Keep the feeling of joy and notice how any negativity is diminished in the presence of joy and light. Go back one more time to the seemingly negative scene and see the joy in it. This is the joy shift.

Now bring that joy with you back into the room, as you become aware of the outer world. Move around and open your eyes and write about your experience with the "Joy Shift."

The more positive energy you can focus on in the face of challenges, the more you'll attract the life you desire to live.

A young girl desired a new bicycle and asked her parents for a new one. They said it would cost more than they had available or even *would* have. The answer was a definite, "no." But the girl paid no attention to that. She saw herself with a new bike. She visualized it. She imagined riding down the street with the breeze against her cheeks as she floated along. Three weeks later, the girl's mother answered the telephone. It was the Supermarket manager telling her that her daughter had won a drawing. The prize? A brand new ten-speed bike!

Keep seeing what you desire. Visualize it. Feel as if it is already so no matter what anyone tells you. It's not hard.

Let's use visualization right now to see yourself being whatever you would like to be or do. Choose one of your goals and let another person read this visualization for you to claim it. Once again, turn within and relax. Follow your breath in and out and fill yourself with light.

Now, see yourself walking up a hillside. Notice nature's beauty around you. The gentle breeze, birds singing, flowers blooming. Take a big deep breath of the fresh air. Eventually you reach the top of the hill. There someone has provided an easel and canvas on which to paint a picture. There are brushes and paints. Move to the easel…pick up a brush and dip it into the paint. You have been given the ability to paint with ease and beauty. So begin to paint a picture on the canvas of a scene in which your goal is accomplished. Include yourself in the picture. Paint all the right colors. Make the scene perfect. (Pause) Add any finishing touches to this painting of the scene where you have reached the goal you had in mind. Stand back and observe your masterpiece. It looks exactly right. The way you would have it be. Say to yourself, "I accept this picture of my goal accomplished. It is mine right now." Now take your painting and travel to a location where you can hang your picture. See yourself moving swiftly to your home or office. Wherever you want to display your picture, go ahead and put it on a wall. Admire your handiwork and again and feel the joy of knowing the real scene is already yours in mind. Now gently come back to the room, become aware of the outer world and open your eyes. Write about your experience and then share it with someone.

You can use visualization for lofty goals or everyday activities. A woman was the Sales Manager for the Silicon Valley company I mentioned on an earlier recording – the one I was guided to create. Anyway, she would sit outside of a business in her car before an appointment and visualize herself walking out with a check and jumping up in the air with joy about her success. It worked some 95% of the time!

You have a powerful tool residing within you. Your mind is always forming pictures and your experiences of life are being created from those pictures. Why not form pictures that you truly desire to experience? It's your choice. Visualize your dreams and accept infinite blessings.

Assignments

1. Read the material, "Growth."

2. Write one "win" daily.

3. Meditate at least sixteen minutes daily. Include "visioning" if you like.

4. Repeat your prosperity affirmation 100 times daily.

5. Write or mind map in your journal on any subject.

6. Read or say a Positive Prayer at least once a day.

7. Visualize a different goal each day.

I know that you are prosperous, guided, and your life is so blessed in every way. You are easily and effortlessly accepting the manifestation of our highest goals and life is good. And so it is.

Chapter 9

"Game Plan"

Principle: Budget, Order and Balance

Tool: Budgeting

Introduction

You might be tempted to skip this chapter, but it is one of the ten principles that will insure prosperity.

Prosperity Principle #9 – "Game Plan"

Someone pointed out that we yell for the Government to balance the budget, then take the last dime we have to make the down payment on a car that will take five years to pay off.

We are funny about planning our finances. Many of us have cringed at the word "budget" for one reason or another. Frequently, when we hear about a budget, it's the nation's budget and our belief system has convinced us that there is only so much to go around. When it comes to creating a budget for ourselves, that negative feeling reveals itself.

In Suze Orman's book, *The 9 Steps to Financial Freedom*, she notes,

> "What prevents you from dealing with your money is not lack of time, but your fear of money."

Let's take a moment to identify some possible fears around money. What attitudes do you hold, or what negative beliefs do you see others holding onto? Possible examples would be: "Fear of being homeless; fear of what people would think if they knew how much money I owed or how much I make; a belief that one is on a limited income; an attitude that everyone is out to get your money." Make a list of fears

NEGATIVE BELIEFS, ATTITUDES OF FEARS ABOUT MONEY

_____
_____
_____
_____
_____
_____
_____
_____
_____
_____
_____
_____
_____

Next make a list of Truths about the negatives you listed. For example, the Truth about people out to get your money might be stated as, "I know I am always protected by the Light of Spirit and no one can harm me or take from me."

As Jesus said,

"And you will know the truth, and that very truth will make you free." - John 8:32

List some Spiritual Truths and share your list with someone.

TRUTHS ABOUT MONEY

_____
_____
_____
_____
_____
_____
_____
_____
_____
_____
_____
_____
_____
_____
_____
_____
_____
_____
_____

So what do we do with these truths now that we have discovered them?

> "Men occasionally stumble over the truth, but most of them pick themselves up and hurry off as if nothing ever happened."
>
> - Winston Churchill (1874-1965)

Here's what you can do to apply the "truth" in your life. Focus on these truths whenever you start to believe in the negative statements. The erroneous "facts" will have no more power because...

> "The truth is more important than the facts."
>
> - Frank Lloyd Wright

Assuming all procrastination is now handled because there is no more fear, let's move into working on a budget or "Game Plan."

Prosperity Tool - Budgeting

Even though you may not have a budget, my guess is that you have some kind of a "game plan." You probably know how much income you'll likely receive this month and you know what bills and expenses you need to pay. It may all be in your head, but you have some plan.

Your plan might be, "work as hard as I can to make as much

money as I can to pay as many bills as I can and have enough to live on." That's a plan. Not the best, perhaps, but it is a plan. The most sophisticated game plan would include not only current revenue and expenses, but plans for future purchases, savings goals, investment plans and retirement plans.

Let's get your game plan on paper. List all the revenue you expect to receive this month. Write the source and the amount, such as:

Paycheck	$2,500
Interest on savings	50
Brother – Loan payback	250
Total Income	$2,750

Then list your expected monthly expenses and add some for unexpected expenses that might come up. Write the expense item and the amount, such as:

Tithe	$ 255
Savings	255
Fun	255
Rent	530
Utilities	200
Taxes	450
Groceries	200
Car payment	225
Gas and service	100
Car Insurance	60
Clothing	50
Life Insurance	70
Credit Card payment	50
Misc.	50
Total Expenses	$2,750

Notice that the projected income and expenses are the same. The paycheck is the gross amount, so taxes are listed under expenses to reflect deductions for Social Security, Federal Taxes and State Taxes. The tithe is calculated on the income only; not on the repayment of a loan. This "game plan" includes one tenth to oneself to have fun and one tenth of the income to savings.

My Monthly Game Plan (Use real amounts to the best of your ability.)

INCOME:

Item	Amount
_____	$_____
_____	_____
_____	_____
_____	_____
_____	_____
_____	_____
_____	_____
TOTAL INCOME	$_____

EXPENSES:

Item   Amount

_____ $_____

_____   _____

_____   _____

_____   _____

_____   _____

_____   _____

_____   _____

_____   _____

_____   _____

_____   _____

_____   _____

_____   _____

_____   _____

_____   _____

_____   _____

TOTAL EXPENSES $_____

DIFFERENCE (Income less Expenses) $_____

What do you do if the expenses exceed income? Remember the importance of order and balance to let expansion happen naturally. Do whatever is necessary to bring balance into your "Game Plan." Either increase your income or reduce your expenses. Then, once you have a balanced "Game Plan," stick to it. Use affirmations and positive prayer to spiritually support yourself in the ability to live your plan. Say something like,

"I plan wisely and God's power provides the strength for me to live my plan."

There are a number of additional categories in which you might desire to have a game plan. What about an extensive retirement plan or a plan for leaving an inheritance? A great resource book for such planning is *The 9 Steps to Financial Freedom* by Suze Orman.

In addition, you might want to create a game plan for how to allocate your time. Start by keeping a time log for two typical weeks. Write down what you did during each fifteen-minute increment of each day. You can use broad categories such as work, sleep, exercise, eating, fun, study, spiritual etc. Add up how many hours you spent in each category out of the 336 hours in the two-week period. For example, if you slept seven hours every night, that would be 98 hours. You can then figure out what percentage of your total time was spent in each activity. (98 divided by 336 = 29%). They say the average American spends seven hours a day watching TV. In that case, you would be spending 29% of your time being a couch potato. Once you have figured out what percentage of time you spend on each category, you can decide if you would like to change it. Let's say you decided to reduce your TV time to two hours a day or 8%. That leaves you with 21% of your day to do something else. That's five hours you could spend meditating each day! See how you're spending your time and change it to align with your goals and priorities. Then, again use spiritual tools to support yourself in sticking with your plan.

Even if you only estimate your "Game Plans" for various areas of your life, it will be a valuable experience. As you pay attention to these matters, you are giving energy to having your life be the way you desire it to be.

Assignment

1. Reread the material, "Game Plan."

2. Write one "win" daily.

3. Meditate at least eighteen minutes daily. Include "visioning" as desired.

4. Repeat your prosperity affirmation 100 times daily.

5. Write in your journal or mind map specifically expressing your feelings about budgeting.

6. Read or say a positive prayer at least once a day.

7. Visualize your life the way you would have it be at least once.

8. Create a "Game Plan."

Chapter 10

"Givingness"

Principle: Tithing Talent and Treasure

Tool: Tithing

Introduction

Last, but certainly not the least important, we explore giving and tithing, reciprocal principles comprising the same energy.

Prosperity Principle #10 – "Givingness"

A young lad was on his way to Sunday school with two quarters in his hand that his parents had given him. One was for the boy and the other was to put in the Sunday school collection basket. As he skipped along the sidewalk, he accidentally dropped the quarters. He picked up one quarter, but the other one rolled into the gutter and down a grate. As he peered down into the dark abyss, he said, "There goes God's quarter!"

Sometimes we act like kids when it comes to giving. If we come from a position of lack and scarcity, we might be tempted to grab what we can and hold on to it tightly. A survival mechanism kicks in and causes us to withhold and draw back. Unfortunately, from a spiritual point of view, such action is the worst thing we could do. We don't serve ourselves or anyone else when we're stingy, miserly or hold a poverty consciousness. When fear causes us to shut down our givingness, we shut down a portion of our aliveness and it can lead to a downward spiral of struggle, strife and unhappiness.

> "A miser is ever in want."
>
> - Greek Proverb

It's been said that when it comes to giving, some people stop at nothing!

And Joseph Murphy commented in his book, *Your Infinite Power to be Rich,*

> "When you mentally wish to withhold wealth from another, you also automatically withhold it from yourself…You are the only thinker in your universe, and your negative thoughts set up negative reactions in all departments of your life."

You can't give anything, without getting something in return. Are you giving what you would like to receive?

Close your eyes for a moment and take a deep breath. Relax. Bring to your mind a time when you gave someone a gift and when they opened it, they were both surprised and thrilled. You felt their genuine gratitude. And you felt great. Pause now to do that brief exercise.

It's true that it's more blessed to give than to receive. The giver receives the real gift....joy.

The Bible is full of teachings about giving. Unfortunately, many people learned to mistrust the Bible because they learned to mistrust some of its adherents. Terry Cole-Whittaker points out,

> "What were meant to be lessons on the truth about not being attached to money or material things became dogma or doctrine about the evils of money, power and things."
>
> - *How to Have in a Have Not World*, Terry Cole-Whittaker

Without turning it into dogma, let's just explore a few relevant passages from ancient scripture. First, there's the idea that we are powerful choice-makers. What we choose is created.

> "Give and it will be given to you; good measure shaken down and running over they will pour into your robe. For with the measure that you measure, it will be measured to you."
>
> - Luke 6:38

Regarding pouring into your robe, Bible scholar George Lamsa pointed out that people living in the Middle East carry wheat from house to house in the folds of their robes. The point remains, you measure out the good that you will receive by what you give.

Jesus told a story that has become known as "The Parable of the Talents" and you can find it in Matthew 25:14-29.

It seems a man went on a journey. Before he departed, he put his servants in charge of his wealth. He gave five talents to one, two talents to another, and one talent to a third man. A talent is believed to have been worth about $1,000 in today's money. The man who was given five talents invested the money and earned five more. The one with two talents did some trading and gained two more talents. But the man with one talent, hid the money in the ground.

When the lord of the servants returned, he asked each how they did. To the first man, he said, "Well done, good and reliable servant. You have been faithful over a little. I will appoint you over much; enter into your master's joy."

When he found out that the second man had doubled the two talents, he again said, "Well done, good and reliable servant. You have been faithful over a little. I will appoint you over much; enter into your master's joy."

The third man explained that he had been afraid, so he hid the money. The master's reaction was: "Oh wicked and lazy servant, you should have put my money in the exchange. Therefore take away the talent from him and give it to the one who has ten talents."

This is a story about the spiritual principal of givingness. Hoarding our gifts diminishes our rewards. Investing our funds by giving multiplies them and good comes back to us.

> "Honor the Lord with your substance and with the first fruits of all your crops; so shall your barns be filled with plenty, and your wine presses shall burst out with new wine."
>
> - Proverbs 3:9-10

It is necessary to our very lives that there be a giving and a receiving; give and take. You must exhale in order to inhale. It's all a part of the natural circulation of life. Someone has said there is one basic problem in life: congestion. There is one basic solution: circulation. Giving brings about circulation and dissolves congestion.

In Catherine Ponder's *The Secret of Unlimited Prosperity,* she tells of a widow who didn't have any money to give. In fact she didn't even have food on her table to feed her children who hadn't eaten since the previous day. She remembered some flowers in her yard, picked them and gave them to a sick neighbor. Then she prepared the dinner table and made out a grocery-shopping list. (Remember, she did all this without having any money.) Soon someone who owed her thirty dollars unexpectedly came by with full payment. Coincidence? I don't think so. When the widow gave away the flowers, she set the Law of Circulation into motion and enjoyed the result.

Givingness and generosity set the Law into motion and return to the giver unlimited blessings.

Prosperity Tool - Tithing

When I was learning the principles of prosperity, I became convinced of the Law of Circulation. I truly believed that giving was vital to experiencing wealth. But I questioned how much to give.

The ancient farmers were advised to set aside one-tenth of the seed from their harvest to plant for the next year's crop. The first born goats and other animals were to be given to God as a gesture of faith.

The earliest reference to giving to one's spiritual Source is found in Genesis 13:2 where Abram, who later was known as Abraham, gives ten percent of everything to Melchizedek. Melchizedek is described as the King of Salem, who was the priest of the Most High. (Genesis 14:20). One tenth is also called a tithe. Tithe means giving a tenth or ten percent of one's income to the Source of their spiritual support and nurturing.

The Bible refers to tithing in several verses including Malachi 3:10:

> "Bring all the tithes into my storehouse that there may be food in my house, and prove me now in this, says the Lord of hosts, and I will open the windows of heaven for you and pour out blessings for you until you shall say, It is enough."

Wondering about that percentage, I researched the writings of Joseph Murphy who wrote that the amount doesn't necessarily have to be one tenth, rather you should give the amount that you can give cheerfully and freely, but not grudgingly or from a sense of duty or fear. He pointed out that the Egyptians gave twenty percent to their temples, the Hebrews gave forty percent even after they were required to pay taxes to the Roman government in New Testament times, and Hindu's required one tenth unless the tithers were poor. In that case, they were required to give twenty percent, because the poor needed to give more to expand their prosperity consciousness.

Still wondering, "Why ten?" my research led me to a couple of resources that convinced me of the validity of giving one tenth.

Albert Pike, who lived in the 1800's and wrote *Morals and Dogma of Freemasonry* in 1870, claimed:

> Ten is the most perfect number because it includes unity, which created everything, and zero, symbol of matter and chaos, whence everything emerged. In its figures it comprehends the created and the uncreated, the commencement and the end, power and force, life and annihilation. By the study of this number, we find the relationships of all things."

Another clarifying viewpoint came from a Religious Science minister, Rev. Arthur Thomas, in his book, *Abundance is Your*

Right. Psychologically, the number ten seems to have deep significance as a number of increase. Apparently, humankind created numbers as picture forms to represent ideas. I believe that at some level, we carry an ancient memory of the symbolic meaning of those numbers. Thomas claims,

> "Ten is a mystical number composed of the upright one and the circular zero representing the male and female characteristics, the union of which is abundantly creative."

The number "1" could represent the Active Spirit and the "0" is the Subjective Mind or Creative Medium. As the Spirit acts upon the Creative Medium, abundant goodness is the result.

The real test of tithing is in the doing. I have tithed for more than a twenty years and I continue to prosper. And I understand that sometimes it's hard to take that leap of faith and try it. That's why I have gradually increased your tithe in this class.

The treasurer of a church used a clever technique. It seems the one treasurer resigned from the Board of Trustees and the Board asked one of the members of the church, the operator of a local grain elevator, to take the position. He agreed under two conditions:

1. That no treasurer's report would be given for one year.
2. That no questions be asked during that year.

Since the people of the church knew him well and trusted him, they agreed. They all had done business with him and knew he was honest.

At the end of the year the new treasurer reported:

> All church indebtedness of $228,000 had been paid.
>
> The minister's salary had been increased by 8%.
>
> There were no unpaid bills.
>
> The cash balance was $11,252.

"How did you do it?" they asked.

"When you brought your grain to me," the treasurer explained, "I withheld 10% each time and gave it to the church in your name. You didn't even miss it."

Here are a few guidelines about tithing:

Donating is not tithing. A donation is something you can spare.

A contribution is not a tithe. A contribution is something included in monthly planning.

Giving because an organization needs it is not a tithe. Giving to need, strengthens need.

Giving to relatives is not a tithe. It's charity.

Giving to charity is not a tithe. Charities aren't your source of spiritual inspiration and nurturing.

Giving to get something back is not a tithe. A tithe is given freely with no strings attached.

Give to what you want to empower.

Give to the persons or organizations, which successfully demonstrate Truth principles.

Give ten percent of your gross income.

If you are self-employed, give ten percent of your draw or your profit from the business.

In a booklet entitled *The Magic of Tithing,* Emmet Fox wrote,

> "The payment of a tithe is an extremely efficient act of faith."

Also be aware that the tithing of your talent is important. Talent does not replace monetary giving. Remember you reap what you sew. If you want financial prosperity, tithe from your finances. Tithing of your talent will bring you many blessings and you'll feel good about it. You were born to express God in some unique way, so don't hold back. Seek ways to give of yourself.

Apply the principle of tithing of your talent and treasure and you will bring showers of blessings upon yourself.

Before we conclude, let's review the ten principles of prosperity.

You might like to rate yourself on the level of mastery in each area in order to determine which principles could use more attention.

Give yourself a "one" for a very low level of mastery of the particular principle and a "ten" for total mastery. If you score 100 overall, you can't help but be the wealthiest person alive! The low scores will tell you areas in which you could improve your prosperity consciousness. Circle where you assess yourself to be on these principles:

God (Rate yourself on how clear you are that God is your Source)
1 2 3 4 5 6 7 8 9 10

Gratitude (How thankful are you? Do you count your blessings?)
1 2 3 4 5 6 7 8 9 10

Guiltless (Do you feel worth to receive God's bounty?)
1 2 3 4 5 6 7 8 9 10

Goodness (Are you convinced that money & prosperity are good?)
1 2 3 4 5 6 7 8 9 10

Gladness (Are you happy in your work or life activities?)
1 2 3 4 5 6 7 8 9 10

Guidance (Are you able to tune in to the highest guidance?)
1 2 3 4 5 6 7 8 9 10

Goals (How clear are you about your intentions and goals?)
1 2 3 4 5 6 7 8 9 10

Growth (Are you aware of the expanding nature of the universe?
1 2 3 4 5 6 7 8 9 10

Game Plan (Do you have balance and order in your finances?)
1 2 3 4 5 6 7 8 9 10

Givingness (Do you tithe of your talent and treasure?)
1 2 3 4 5 6 7 8 9 10

Total Score: _____

Congratulations!

Even though the book is ending, I'd like to give you some assignments.

Assignments

1. Reread class #10 "Givingness."

2. Write some wins every day of your life.

3. Meditate at least 20 minutes daily from now on.

4. Use the other tools you've learned in this book on a regular basis.

5. Tithe ten percent of your "treasure" and tithe of your talents as well.

Have a prosperous life. I know that you are prosperous, guided, and your life is so blessed in every way. I accept the out-picturing of your highest intentions.

As you easily and effortlessly apply the 10 principles of prosperity, you reap the benefits of abundance and success. This is the Mystical 10.

And so it is.

www.ingramcontent.com/pod-product-compliance
Lightning Source LLC
Chambersburg PA
CBHW041617220426
43671CB00004B/46